Why I Run

~ my story of how I own my life back from the darkness of depression ~

Darcy Patrick

Tellwell Talent
www.tellwell.ca

ISBN
978-1-77302-219-2 (Paperback)
978-1-77302-220-8 (eBook)

Special thank to Patrick Brown for editing and inspiring me with writing.

Contents

Foreword

This book is about a man's continuing struggle with depression and his healing journey. It is about the steps he went through to regain control over his life after struggling for many years.

"Why I Run" is a book written not only for individuals with depression, but also for their families and friends. Unlike many books on depression, this book has the authenticity derived from being written by someone who experienced it firsthand.

Depression does not discriminate. It can be experienced by anyone regardless of their age, socioeconomic background, culture, education or gender. However, the societal stigma attached to this illness has made it a taboo to acknowledge. It is this power that prevents people from seeking professional help, or even just talking about it with a friend.

Depression is not having the blues, nor is something you just shake off or snap out of. It can control you physically and mentally. It stops people from moving forward in their lives and reaching their full potential. It takes courage to seek help and openly talk about one's experiences.

As a Clinical Therapist, I have come across many amazing people, like Darcy, whose lives have been consumed by depression.

In some ways Darcy's journey is both common and uncommon. It is common in that so many people struggle with depression, but uncommon as he falls in the small percentage who seeks help. It is even more uncommon in that he had the courage to write about it and share his experiences openly with the world.

Therapy is not what is portrayed in pop culture, where people simply talk and therapists offer advice. It is an intensive process that relies on open communication between the therapist and the client.

The therapist draws from a variety of therapies and tailors them to the individual's circumstances in the form of a treatment plan. But most importantly, the client must commit to the treatment plan. The real work through commitment and resilience happen outside therapy sessions.

Through Darcy's treatment plan we figured out that Darcy responded best to Cognitive Behavioural Therapy (CBT) and Eye Movement Desensitization Reprocessing (EMDR).

CBT helps individuals to become aware of their negative thinking, look at the problems in a new way, have a new understanding of the problem in more effective way. It gives an individual the skills to address their issues they are presently dealing with it.

EMDR is non-traditional psychotherapy that helps individuals to process and heal from the symptoms resulted from disturbing life experiences. It was originally developed in 1987 by Francine Shapiro to treat Post-traumatic Stress Disorder (PTSD). Since then, it has been used to effectively treat a wide range of mental health problems (depression, anxiety, grief etc).

When I first met Darcy, he did not believe that he could lead a normal life or that therapy could help him. He struggled in the beginning. And like most first timers was cautious about sharing too much with a stranger.

Once he started to open up, we spent many sessions building his confidence, developing coping strategies and restructuring his negative thinking pattern using CBT and Mindfulness. He was given homework at the end of each session which helped Darcy work on his issues between the sessions. The first goal was to stabilize Darcy and to help him to cope with his daily life. Once this was done we could begin addressing his past traumas through EMDR.

When I first discussed EMDR with Darcy, he was hesitant. He worried that dealing with past would take him back into the darkness of depression. Therefore we spent a lot of time in the EMDR preparation phase before moving forward with the assessment phase. Even during the first couple of sessions of assessment phase, Darcy struggled to trust the process as he feared facing his past. However, once he reprocessed his first trauma, he let go of his fear and successfully completed EMDR treatment plan. His traumas no longer haunt him.

Darcy does all this and beyond as you will see in this book. As he progressed through his treatment plan he developed a toolbox of coping strategies to help him with every day challenges and manage his depression overall. The stronger his tool box became, the weaker his depression. Darcy's consistent resilience transforms him into a confident person who learns to take control of his life, his present and his future.

This book will show that over the course of Darcy's treatment, his opinion changes considerably about therapy and depression.

Ultimately this book has two purposes. First, to prove to you that depression is treatable if you get the right help. There is no quick fix but requires consistency, dedication and hard work to feel better. Second, that it demonstrates how to take control over your life and not let depression dictate your present or future.

In short, remember one important point from this book---self-care defeats depression and letting go of self-care strengthens depression. Seeking counselling is a sign of strength. No matter what the issue, therapy can help.

I commend Darcy for sharing his experiences with the world and bringing this illness to forefront.

Mastora Roshan, MSW. RSW.
Clinical Therapist
Therapeutic Solutions Counselling
St. Catharines, Ontario

Intro

I have gone 38 years living and only thinking about what people think of me. I don't want anyone to think or know I'm crazy

I'm embarrassed because I'm crazy. I feel that I'm a burden on my friends if I talk to them and tell them how I feel.

Friends and other people would always ask me, in a smart-ass way, two questions about why I run...

Where are you running to?

What are you running from?

These questions used to bother me. I would lie and say things like, I run to lose weight, or, I am running from fat. When I was being kind of a smart-ass myself, and felt like speaking a half-truth, I would say I am running from myself.....

The first step

When I ran I used to think about all the bad things in my life. I used to worry about debt, about how much money I owed and how I was going to lose my house. How much of a failure I was because of this debt I owed..... I would think about work and repairs I had fucked up and how many people disliked me because of those mistakes I had made....I also would think about how much of a loser I was, always failing and never succeeding in life at all... Failing to get pregnant and finding out I had CF just amplified my failures.

I wasn't running from myself or fat or anything like that. I was beating myself up... over time I started to punish myself and run longer and longer and longer in hopes my body would break, in hopes that I would just run myself into the ground. 5km turned to 8km to 10km to 12 to 14 to 16, all along just thinking about all this bad shit never enjoying any of this time to myself...

Then came the 21 km runs. I would run 4 a year. Extra-long runs of hate.

My runs of hate I call them now. My runs of hate happened 5 days a week, topping out at 50 km per week. I was so broken inside, spiraling down every day. Dark places and dark thoughts crept in, like wishing I would disappear.....In other words, die. I wanted to run until I died.

I tried and tried, but my body just took it, more and more, getting stronger and thinner and able to run longer and longer, till a 16 km run was like a walk in the park...... no matter what I did my body wouldn't break and so my depression just kept on beating me up.......... 38 years easy of self-hate.

Run after run, morning after morning I built up a vast amount of self hate.... All my short-comings...

- Infertility
- Failing at work
- Debt
- Failing RCMP and police tests
- Missing out on things when I was young
- Worrying about what people thought about me.
- Worrying about making people happy
- Worrying about my bank account
- Worrying about no gigs coming in

I would run through all this shit, the whole run every day, over and over again, just beating myself up for an hour or more.

One day I was in the darkest place I have ever been. CF and Infertility had taken their pieces of me after artificial insemination failed five times. We were in the middle of three years of waiting for adoption...

I reached the end. I got up. I ran 14 km and beat myself up real bad. I got to an overpass over the highway. I stopped dead. I took a deep breath. I placed my hands on the railing. I was ready to jump. But something stopped me.

I couldn't do it. I just ran away.......

That day at work we got the call!!! That day I met my son Dylan!!! It was one of the happiest days of my life...just writing this now brings tears to my eyes. I was so happy and over-joyed when I first laid eyes on him it was electric. His eyes met mine and we bonded in that second. It was the most magical thing that has ever happened to me in my life. And to think that eight hours earlier I was standing on an overpass ready to jump. End it all and never meet this little man that I will now have a lifelong adventure with, growing and learning and loving each day with him. The end.

No, depression just doesn't go away. It has to be fought off every day. I would have loved to say that meeting him flipped a switch inside and turned my inner darkness and self-hate and worry off. Switched off my constant thoughts of failure and how much of a waste of flesh I am. But that didn't happen.

There is a song I play in a band that is called *Lovers in a Dangerous Time*, by Bruce Cockburn. When I play this song it strikes me in the heart, I feel so alive and real. When I play it, I put all my emotion and creativity in to it. When I play it, I get lost in the moment and feel free.

Why? There is a line in the song which I sing all the time that anyone who suffers from depression would identify with.

"Nothing worth having doesn't come without some kind of fight... you got to kick at the darkness till it bleeds day light"....

Beating depression is a learning process. There is no magic pill, no switch, No just seeing a therapist once. It's hard work.

So I still ran with hate, still running from my past, from things that happened to me that I thought were unfair and tragic. Still trying my best to run further and further, thinking it is so much easier to run and hide things than it is to fight... just like that song lyric. I chose to run, not to fight, run and hate and worry and think about bad things. Beat myself up. Each step, each foot hitting the ground, each deep breath I took when I ran, purely centered and making its mark, to self-loathe and self-hate.

But when I got home I became another person. There was a switch I would throw. I could hide my depression better than anyone. While I am a total mess, I am playing with my son. I am having dinner with friends. Doing a gig with a band. Just acting, like no one else ever could. On the outside I am Darcy Patrick, husband, father, musician, salesman, repair man, amp tech, shipper, receiver, manager, you name it... But really I am falling apart, crying and hating myself, and just wanting to disappear.

I was the greatest actor ever, better than Harrison Ford, better than anyone, you name it. I would win the Oscar every time!

I could never let my wife Sherri down, or my beautiful son Dylan. I could never show weakness.

I would smile and play the game and all along just be beating myself up and hiding the total emotional breakdown I was in every day, just smiling and acting and dying slowly inside...running and running from my past. Running from myself... and acting each day. Getting stronger physically and weaker and weaker emotionally.

I started crying all the time: while I was running, when I was alone in my office at work, downstairs at home playing my bass, outside gardening. My hands would shake, my heart would race, my emotions would go from 0 -100 in seconds. I would feel hopeless and trapped. Spiraling down, I call it.

I see no way out. Blinders go on. The world closes in. I am alone and humiliated, embarrassed, a failure, a waste of flesh. All I want is to disappear, to kill myself. Darkness was always over my shoulder just waiting to pounce, but it has a funny way of just dragging you down, till you have no choice but to confront it. One day I did...

One day I stopped working on a guitar. My friend and co-worker came into the room and said to me "That is it you are calling someone right now and I am not letting you work on another guitar or leave this room till you do". It was time. I was finished. I couldn't last any longer.

I walked over to my computer and I Googled "depression therapist in St Catharines". I looked at the listing and found a woman whose profile I read and liked. I called her and made an appointment for the next day.

The running was over it was time to fight and win my life back from the darkness....

When I walked into my first appointment I was terrified! What was going to happen? What was I going to talk about? How could this help me...? Was I just supposed to start talking to this stranger and tell her things that I have never told anyone before? What was the deal here... how could she help me? I was so broken and depressed, how could she put me back together?

She talked to me, asked me what brought me there and told me I was not a failure, that I made a huge step just calling and showing up. She told me I was worth changing and that she could help me and teach me that I could beat depression....I believed her and I talked for the first time.

I told her how empty I was and how I wanted to disappear sometimes. About how much acting I did and how I was such a failure.

She told me that I have been putting all my feelings and emotions into a barrel and it was full to over flowing and there is this beach ball that is getting pushed down into the barrel and my emotions are all over flowing over the sides, out of control. She told me how she was going to change my way of thinking and my way of dealing with life, and we were going to drain that barrel and start living life!!

I clearly remember the run I had the next day. Instead of beating myself up that morning, I thought about everything she said and I actually felt that she was right. I wasn't a failure and if she was right about that, then maybe I am worth changing and I don't want to disappear after all and maybe, just maybe, I can learn something from these sessions, and if I work hard enough and fight I will beat this depression and stop spiraling down someday.

Now this was a run of hope and happiness, a run to start a new outlook on life, maybe just be myself!!! I deserve to be happy!!

This is my story of beating depression, how I stopped running from myself, and how I started living life and learning so much about myself!

This is what I wrote in my journal that day.

I had questions

I had questions. Strange ones. Now I know the answers. But I had trained myself in a way of thinking that these questions were very important and needed to be answered.

1. Do people take joy in doing simple things? Is it right for me to actually do something and get lost in the moment and truly enjoy myself or is it a totally selfish thing to do? Do normal people do this all the time?
2. Is it okay to let go of things that I have done and things that have been done to me? Is it okay to completely move on in life and not relive events and stew about them over and over again?
3. Is it completely okay if I just give up on people and let them fade into the past? Not thinking about them all the time and just live and let die, per se?
4. If I do let go and go to this safe place and just cry and finally let my emotions go will that be completely wrong because a safe place is supposed to be somewhere peaceful and if I let go and cry it really isn't peaceful, is it??? Will I go completely crazy if I do let go 100%? Will I be better or worse for showing my emotions?

These questions were so real to me I needed to know the answers..... Now when I look back at them, I realize that I was so, so lost then.

Question 1: Do people take joy in doing simple things? Is it right for me to actually do something and get lost in the moment and truly enjoy myself or is it a totally selfish thing to do? Do normal people do this all the time?

The big one. I couldn't grasp the concept of just enjoying myself. After all, I ran every day and I never enjoyed myself. I played in a band, but never enjoyed myself. I played my bass, practised 4 hours a day, never enjoyed myself.

What a strange thing, actually enjoying one self. I had trained myself for so long to live for other people and not myself so even just doing anything nice for myself seemed like a selfish act. So I gave it a try. Why not?

My therapist told me to start doing something for myself. So I listened, and learned that everything takes practice, even enjoying yourself. I started going for coffee at a nice little coffee shop on the way to work. I would just sit there and think about nothing. It was so hard at first, but I got better at it and before I knew it my day just didn't feel right unless I went there either before work or at lunch.

I practised treating myself well, till it felt good. Such a small thing, just having a coffee and not thinking. Just taking joy in doing nothing. The world can wait for Darcy Patrick for once. He is having a coffee and enjoying himself!

I started watching my son. I coloured with him, played Lego with him, and learned so much from him. Children know how to get lost in the moment. Getting lost in the moment is not easy for a depressed person.

"I love playing Lego with my son."

My son would take a Lego man and stand him on a small brick and the Lego man had a jet pack, he was flying around the room. Put that same Lego man on a bigger piece of Lego, he is surfing. Add wheels to that surf board you have a skate board. Getting lost in play with a 5 year old is priceless.....you just play, no one saying that what you're doing is wrong. You're just playing, having fun.

There is nothing wrong with getting lost and enjoying the moment. Small things are great to get lost in.

Stop and smell the roses, people say sometimes. I used to just laugh and think who has time for that! And I love gardening! But I never took the time to smell the roses. I would use my gardening time like I did my running time: for self-hate and loathing.

But now I was learning that it is okay to get lost. It's okay to enjoy yourself. It's okay to love the moment you are in, and I don't care what normal people do because no one is normal and now I can do whatever I want to do. Just as long as I think it is good, then, man, it is good.

Living for other people and depending on their happiness for my own happiness was a dead end street. It left me broken and battered and depressed the answer to question number 1 was, Yes. Yes to everything and that is it.

Question 2: Is it okay to let go of things that I have done. And things that have been done to me? Is it okay to completely move on in life and not relive them and stew about them over and over again?

"I hold on to things I keep them alive for an extreme amount of time."

If I felt something was bad and was against me I would stay in that moment and just relive it over and over again. I had a file folder of tragic things, a pretty large one.

The things I thought were tragic, I felt by keeping them alive and reliving them all the time I could change them... But keeping them alive just brewed hate and self-loathing. So all these life experiences got amplified over time and they got stronger and stronger with every run. I would not let anything slide in life. Nothing ever just went in one ear and out the other. Never, ever did I let something not bother me.

Retraining and learning to actually heal these things was a huge task and I had no idea where I would start and I had to heal and move on because life is way too short not to have new experiences and fun.

Staying in a moment and living in the moment are two different things and just dedicating all this time to bad shit just is a waste of time. Time goes by too fast and not letting go and healing things that happened when you were a child and in grade school or a teenager or an adult or even something that happened last week or yesterday is bad...

So you have to let these things go. So yes, it is okay. I will talk more about how I learned to do this later on in the book. But answer Number 2 is Yes...

Question 3: Is it completely okay if I just give up on people and let them fade into the past? Not thinking about them all the time and just live and let die, per se?

I tried to change people by thinking of them and their actions. Instead of figuring out a way to talk to people I work with I would force my work ethic on them and when it didn't take I would stew about it and lose sleep. This transferred to everything I was having problems with and on a personal level it was even worse.

I have friends that I haven't talked to in a while and I will not let it go. I constantly think of them and beat myself up thinking I must have done something wrong and then Bang! I am trying to figure out a way to make them happy so I can feel better about myself. I just wouldn't let things go ever. People just grow apart for no apparent reason sometimes, but try telling me that. Noooo, I can fix it. I bend my own self to make amends and I have to be friends with everyone and everyone has to like me.....

It was so wrong of me to be like this and it was bred into me growing up in a house of six older brothers and seeing the infighting and the fights in general. I watched and learned bad things. I tried to be liked by all my brothers, just bending and bending all the time never, ever living for myself, just fearing that someone might not like me...

Letting friends and even family go their own way is a good thing. Realizing that you don't have to live your life to keep friends and family is very important. It is good to remember good times and learn from them. It is great to have friends and it is also alright to grow apart. Believe it or not, it is okay to have people not like you. That's just the way it is. Letting some people fade away and just be an old friend is fine.

So 'live and let die' is fine. Holding on to friends meant not being able to move forward in life. That's a bad thing. Learn to put your life first, your own feelings, your own emotions, your own goals, and your own family. Your wife, your son, and you – most important of all is you! Because how can your wife and son actually learn and love and grow if you aren't there for them in mind and body 100%, not acting but truly there?

Let people go. Let them grow and if you meet in the middle even after 20 years you will still be happy to see them. Answer 3 is Yes. Live and let die. Let people go!!!! It hurts, sometimes for a long time, but just let it go. Hurting is part of healing.

Question 4: If I do let go and go to this safe place and finally let my emotions go will that be completely wrong – because a safe place is supposed to be somewhere peaceful and if I let go and cry it really isn't peaceful, is it? Will I go completely crazy if I do let go 100%? Will I be better or worse for showing my emotions?

A safe place....... well a safe place is just what it is: safe. Safe for whatever you want it to be. When I wrote these questions my therapist was so concerned for my wellbeing. I would not take meds to level myself out, so we tried installing a safe place for me to go to. We tried meditation, just relaxing and doing nothing, getting away from all these bad thoughts. Then, when I would start spiraling down, I could take a moment to relax and just go to this place and let the world pass me by just for a moment.

But the problem was everything I chose I over-analyzed and turned it into a source of stress, something that was a big, big mess.

I remember running one morning and thinking, this safe place will never come. It is just a waste of time for me and really this whole trying to get better altogether was a waste of time and money. I'll never get it, never get it. But I did and I have a safe place and I cry there, I laugh there, and I celebrate it! I go there all the time. A safe place is just what it says it is: a safe place to go to and it doesn't matter what you do there.

A safe place…

Finding my safe place

Journal entry:

I need to talk to my therapist about why I can't let go of my emotions why I just can't be free from my thoughts. How there are always things on my mind. I never truly relax and just let go.

I am afraid when I do I'll just cry and cry and cry, and just explode with emotion. I have already done that when I wasn't even close to being completely relaxed? What's going to happen to me when I truly let go and let my emotions free after all these years? I am scared and terrified of that moment. I need to feel. I need to be free. I need to let go. I need to be me!! I need to go to this safe place and just let whatever happens happen.

What will happen? I am scared.

I was still spiraling and my therapist wanted to install a safe place that I could go to in my head, like a kind of meditation, to calm me down and make me stable again. Somewhere I could just be at peace.

Now the struggle started. I was so nervous about it I could not relax at all. I was convinced that it was just not going to happen. I could never create a safe place.

It was up to me to find my safe place, so I started.

Attempt #1

I pictured myself walking Moe my dog who I have recently put sleep to the park, us playing Frisbee .The sun was shining and there were pine trees lining the right side of the park and I could smell the morning dew and Moe was running and catching the Frisbee. I could feel the grimy dog saliva on my hand from throwing the Frisbee. I could hear Moe's teeth bite down and catch it as I threw it.

But picturing that didn't work. I could not go there. I could not relax and really I wasn't over Moe at all. The experience was a total disaster. I just broke down and was a mess. I was failing at another thing in life: I was not able to install a safe place and I had never come to grips with putting my dog to sleep....

So it was back to the drawing board for Round 2 at the safe place...

Attempt #2

This time I was at the beach sitting on a beach chair and the sun was shining. It was hot. I was having a beer and the water was just washing up on the shore, nice and calm. My son Dylan was swimming and my wife Sherri was beside me. It was great my therapist was able to bring me there without a problem at all. But the last time I was at the beach was when I had just started therapy and I had a major break down and I ended up just thinking about that day and again I broke down and was a mess once again. I was a failure all over again.

Here is the Journal entry from that time at the beach when I actually broke down.

Journal entry:

At the beach

I hate my life. I'm trying to get better but wife Sherri is so angry and hates me for what I'm going through. What's the use anyway? I'm just going to keep living the way I'm living, unhappy and acting the whole time. So I don't hurt her and Dylan.

That day at the beach I fell apart in front of Sherri, tears and everything. She saw me at the worst.

I was going to break for real. I told her that sometimes I wish I was gone. I wish I would disappear. I told her that I'm not happy, that I have been acting for years and that I'm going crazy. I just fell apart. I was crying and shaking and I just spiraled down. What a way to spend our last days of vacation.

Attempt #3

So now it was time again to try something new. But my therapist just wanted to work on relaxation in general and so she introduced me to the tree meditation, which is one of my favourite things to do. I sit and breathe deep and just feel how my body is sitting and just notice everything that is around me. I close my eyes and just breathe deeply. She asks me what kind of tree I see before me. I tell her I see a large brown maple tree. I walk toward this tree and I magically just step into it and just breathe, breathe deeply. I slowly bring the air in through the leaves and push it down through my trunk and out into the ground through my roots and then in through my roots and out through my leaves. I just imagine I can feel the wind blowing me from side to side and I let my body move freely as this tree, just feeling relaxed and peaceful. She asks me what I am feeling, what emotions are flowing through me and I tell her and she just says go with that feeling and enjoy it for as long as you like. Then when you are feeling just right take a deep breath and step out of the tree and open your eyes slowly and stay in that emotion you were feeling. I open my eyes and step out and I am relaxed and at peace and holly smokes I feel so good.

Guess what? I found my safe place and it was fantastic!

I have grown the tree meditation into a beautiful, safe place. I go there all the time. It is so peaceful and I don't cry. I feel free and I can do whatever I like and I just step into a tree.

The tree is a perfectly safe place. When I need to go there, I walk around the tree and run my hand over its bark, feeling its roughness and its nooks and crannies, and kind of say "Hi" to this tree. I imagine that I have this gift and I just slowly walk into this tree and I feel its whole circulatory system and as I breathe I take the air in through the leaves and out through the roots. I feel the sap coursing through my limbs and I imagine the wind blowing my leaves around. I just feel everything the tree feels, like birds landing on me and even building nests and having baby birds living on me. I stay in the tree till I feel I have stayed long enough and whatever caused me to be stressed out has left my mind. The outside world can't touch me here. I am free from everything in the tree and that is so, so special.

When I walk out, I thank the tree and I give it a nice pat and once again rub my hand along its trunk to feel its bark and roughness. I walk away relaxed and complete and I take the tree's strength with me as I leave my special safe place.

I had over analyzed the safe place till I was terrified of it and I had all these expectations and worries about what a safe place was. A safe place is just that a safe place end of story no over thinking and I can cry I can feel whatever I want to it's my safe place!

Thank you, Mastora, for my safe place.

Journal entry:

Practice, practice, practice.

The more I keep practising all that I am learning, the more I realize that I am getting stronger. Practice, practice, practice. Just like music, it's all about practice... With music, after a long time you can just play. In this case, practice lets you start living life. Learning to let things go is starting to feel right. Treating myself like a human being who deserves to be happy and deserves to be treated nicely is starting to feel good.

Thought records

Thought records are a way of proving yourself wrong. You write down your thoughts at that time, acknowledging what is making your moods go a certain way, and then for each line you write you counter it with a real thought that proves that what you're thinking is actually wrong.

Below is the thought record I had after we tried installing my safe place for the first time.

Thought record:: I went to therapy

Situation::

I went to therapy and it was going well. We tried to create a safe place. I broke down crying and was just a complete mess.

Mood::: Scared 80%, Sad 100%, Distressed100%

Thoughts::::

I'm useless I will never get better. I'm better off dead.

I'm not useless. I passed level 2 training at work. I can do a thought record. I'm a good father and husband. I help people every day.

Why could I not do this? I feel I can never do anything right.

I do things right all the time. I do all the shipping and receiving at work. They trust me with that and I do it well. I'll be able to do create a safe place next time.

Mood::: relaxed 100%

Here is how I do thought records. I learned from my therapist and from a book called *Mind Over Mood*, then I tweaked it a little and made it my own and you can do the same if you like because there is no right or wrong way to do a thought record. It's a tool and you can use the tool anyway you like just as long as it works. Here is how I do it.

1st—The title. I like to do a title to a thought record because it makes it easy to go back and find what I was having a problem with and it helps to clarify what I was actually thinking at the time when I started to spiral or just get upset over something. So here is a kind of fun title I will use to demonstrate a thought record:

Thought record:::: Moe going poop on a walk.

2nd—The situation (or use a short form, as I do, and just write SIT::). Then I write down what happened. I don't express any emotions here. I just write down what happened plain and simple. Just the actual situation, nothing else.

SIT:: I took my dog Moe for a walk and it was a sunny day and we got to a corner and he went up to a tree and took a poop and I had no bag to pick up his mess.

3rd—Now I write down the moods I'm feeling at that time, how this situation made me feel and how strong this feeling was. I use percentages, rating the mood's strength from 0 to 100.

Moods::: Embarrassed 100% Ashamed 100%

4th—Now here is the fun part: the thoughts you have, the emotions that triggered you, the stuff that you think in whatever situation you are in. This is the hard part because you actually have to write down the truth! You have to, because otherwise the thought record will not work. I found this to be so hard because I actually had to feel the emotions, not block them. I had to own up to what I was thinking when this situation was happening. No acting here, but 100% honesty.

It is hard work because we feel that what we are thinking when we are triggered is the truth and that our thoughts are right. Why wouldn't they be? We are always right in our thoughts and feelings!

Wrong!

When you are depressed you have taught yourself bad habits and bad thoughts and now you have to own up to them and prove yourself wrong. My therapist always told me try to think of it as, you are helping out a friend and they came to you with these thoughts and need help. You would help a friend if they came to you with a problem. People do it all the time. So do I. I will give my friends the best advice ever and not even think about it. But try doing it to yourself. Try to explain to a depressed man or woman that their thinking is wrong. Good luck! But here we go. We're going to do it and it takes practice, a lot of practice and a lot of repeating, over and over, thought record after thought record. I will talk about thought records in this book a lot. They're a huge tool and learning to use this tool is key.

Thought:::

I am ashamed of myself because Moe pooped on a tree and I have no bag to clean it up. The owner of the house is on his front porch, watching, and I am so ashamed of myself for not having a bag

Here is my counter thought:

I shouldn't be ashamed. It is a nice sunny day and I was in a hurry to get outside and forgot to bring a bag with me. There is no shame in what has happened here at all. I am human. I forget things.

This is horrible. This man is watching me and I don't have a bag. He knows I live around the corner and now he will see me all the time and think of me as the guy who never cleans up his dog's poop! How will I ever walk down this street again? What a loser I am::::::

Counter thought:

I am not a loser, and I can just come back and pick up the poop later. I am not a bad man. Give me a break here. All I did was leave some dog poop beside a tree. I can walk down the street anytime I like. Who cares if one day I didn`t clean up poop right away? I`ll come back.

It's as easy as that.

So that is an example of a thought record that one is pretty straight-forward, but do you see how I countered my thoughts and made myself feel better and see the situation for what it really was? I had to be honest here. I had to feel no shame in forgetting a little plastic bag. I had to accept that I am human and I make mistakes. Changing the way you think is not easy at all when you are depressed. You think you are always 100% correct and that the situation you are in is 100% real, but it isn`t, not at all and only practising these thought records over and over and over again will change the way you think. I am telling you, kicking at the Darkness till it bleeds day light is a constant fight.

I also have quick thought records where I leave the top part out and just prove myself wrong. I do these records when I am in a tight spot and I do not have time to do the whole thing. When I am at work or at a gig between sets or in a social situation, if I feel the trigger I write it down and then prove it wrong.

I will be posting a lot of real dark thought records some with good comebacks to prove myself wrong and some for which I just didn't have a comeback at all. Some thought records describe real good moments where I had a break through, or a good day. But there really aren't good or bad thought records themselves – they're just thought records. Just writing out things helps a great deal.....just actually writing out your thoughts and then being able to say them and to talk to someone about what you are really feeling will come in time with practice, practice, practice. Lots of writing and proving yourself wrong..

Journals

I also do journal entries. These are just feelings and thoughts that happen throughout the day. If I have a good day, I will write about it. I will say "I am having a good day" because of this or that. It's nice to go back and read about things that happen to you that you loved or made you happy. Maybe they will help you again later on when you are down and need cheering up. You might have gone out with your wife and had a super fun time. Write it down. You deserve to be happy. Celebrate it!! You went to the park and played with your son – write it down and remember it and smile when you read it back someday. It's okay to be happy.

Write down something you thought was beautiful at one time. If you were walking by a house that had the most beautiful flowers in its front yard garden and the colours just blew you away, write it down and read it later! That is practice at living in the moment!! Journals are wonderful things to keep and you have to keep them. They are a tool and they work.

Kicking at the darkness.

Every day is a challenge and every day is a fight to change thought patterns.

I was taught to do thought records to start acknowledging what would trigger me into a spiral and write it down and prove that thought wrong. At first it was really hard because I was 100% sure that I was right about my thinking, but then I started doing what I was told and writing. It was like practising my bass. I spent endless hours playing scales, studying scales, learning how to use these scales to improvise walking bass lines. I went to college for music and I worked my ass off to become the best I could.

I wrote and I wrote and wrote. I was doing five thought records a day and I got to be really good at them. I was seeing what was bothering me and it was shocking at times, my sideways way of thinking. I remember on a gig I was playing one night, after I played a solo, the guitar player saying to me "Darcy that was a great solo, the best you have played on that song." And anyone who wasn't depressed would have taken that compliment and said thank you and would have been happy! Nooo not me instead of being happy and taking it I spiraled down to the bottom right away and I just sank deep, deep, deep.

My thoughts were, I have been playing this tune for years and no one has ever complimented me before does this mean I have been playing shitty for those years? Does it mean the hundreds of times I have soloed on that song before I sucked? What a horrible thing to say to me. It was a complete insult and maybe I am a bad bass player after all. If I only soloed well just that one time on a song I have been playing for years. That is a sign I should pack it in. I always thought I played well on that song. I am such a loser for thinking I am good and I can play music. I should just stop playing and disappear!!! That easily I spiraled down to wanting to disappear! Let's just say the rest of the gig was a wash-out for me. I played well. I acted like Darcy Patrick, the professional bass player and musician, but really I was a total waste of time and space.

I couldn't take a complement no matter what the situation. I went back and started reading my records and true enough I would spiral even after a very true complement I deserved.

So I had to start saying, "Thank you," and leaving it at that. Just accept the compliment, and no matter what my old thought would have been, I just said thank you!!! It was hard work. Changing my thought patterns wasn't easy and still isn't. I love proving myself wrong now and I am good at it. Just like walking over chord changes with my bass, it takes practice, practice... kicking at the darkness till it bleeds daylight takes practice, practice.

Knowing the triggers and stopping them is a major thing and just doing that is a key to beating depression. Sooner or later you just are able to kill the trigger dead and may not even have to do a thought record at all. But I still, to this day, use thought records and Journal entries to help. I like writing and expressing myself. Here are some examples of Journal entries and Thought records

Journal entry:

I'm going to try being myself today! I am going to stand up for myself if I have to. I'm going to speak my mind if I have to, and be happy!

I'm starting out good at the coffee shop!!

Just because I have a few bad days doesn't mean I am stuck again. It doesn't mean I have to stay that way.

What happened yesterday and the day before that is in the past and the past can't be changed and it is gone so I can let it go! I can be like normal people. I answer to me and no one else when it comes to being who I am.

Journal entry:

Some bad days

8:30 am. I'm feeling down. I don't get it. Yesterday was a great day and today the emptiness is surrounding me. I just feel numb and on the edge. I know it's creeping up on me and it's going to grab me.

4:30 it grabs me. I want to walk out of work. I want to disappear again. My heart is racing. I feel every beat and I'm trying to calm down but nothing is working. I'm spiraling down slowly and the feeling of being trapped is growing more and more. What is going on with me? I would do a thought record .But I don't know what to do right now?

Where to start...

I didn't run this morning because I couldn't sleep and if I ran it was one of those mornings where I would have run myself into the ground and not stopped, so I stayed home. I am spinning right now, thinking I'm really getting sick of myself, sick of not being happy and not succeeding and just being me. I wish I could get this over with.

A failure. I'm starting to wish I was just not here anymore again. I'm crying and I'm feeling helpless right now. I walked out of work today, made it to the sidewalk and then I turned around. Just helpless right now.

Didn't run again today because I'm afraid I'll do myself in. My body takes everything I throw at it and I'm going to hurt myself. I'm like a roller coaster. I feel every heart beat and my hands are shaking. I want to run. I want to run for a long time, run till I drop. I ask myself, if I go totally nuts and snap will I finally be able to be myself and be happy and not care about what people think anymore and live for myself? What if I just let go and let it happen ...

Thought record:

2013::

Sit:

2013 was a fucked up year. My job changed in a huge way. I left a band that I thought I was going to be in for my whole life. I pretty much fell apart at the seams and came to grips with the truth that I suffer from depression and put together a new band with good friends.

Moods:

Sad 80%, Anxious 60%, Afraid 80%, Hopeful 100%.

Thoughts:

My job changed.

I adapted to it. I took on more jobs, more responsibility, and I am doing a good job.

I left the band.

I stood up for myself. I left for good reasons. They let me walk and I realize that it was for the best.

I fell apart and the stress from work and the band got the best of me.

I learned that I have a real good friend in Nelson and he pretty much saved me.

I am depressed

I went for help I called a therapist and I got help. She has helped me so much and still is helping me. Without the tools she gave me, I don't know what I would have done. I was on the edge and most likely wouldn't be here right now if not for her. I have a long way to go but now I know I can overcome and get better and feel good a day at a time. That's all I can do. I have been living my life for so long for other people and I have to start now for myself.

New band

The new band is good but I feel like I may need to stop playing and dedicate more time to my own personal health. But maybe music is the key. Who knows?

Here is a good example of proving myself wrong with a thought record.

Thought record:

I'm useless and worthless...

Sit:

We're broke. I can't provide for my family. No matter what I do we can never get ahead. We live in overdraft and we can never get out. The line of credit is almost used up.

Moods:

Sad 100%, Depressed 100%, Embarrassed 100%, Humiliated 90 %

Thoughts:

I work and work but it is not enough I need to work more I need more money

Times are tough and I'm lucky to have a job, never mind stash money away and get ahead.

I haven't even saved for Dylan's education

I have a mutual fund I have been putting money into, and I am saving and once the house is paid for I'll be able to save for his education.

I am lucky to have job! Many people in St Catharines have no job and are on welfare.

I am depressed But still working. Many people like me are stuck at home in bed and never leave the house.

I'm getting better and stronger and I will survive this and I will save and I will make money!

I will beat this. I am not useless! I work hard. I'm not worthless. People rely on me and people need me. I am liked and loved by my wife and son and friends and family! Times are tough but I'm tougher than the times and I will overcome.

The vault

I remember the anxiety I had walking to my therapist the morning I decided to talk about the vault.

I ran that morning, thinking if I was going to get better I really wanted to talk about the vault and I was so, so nervous about it and about the stuff I had in the vault.

The vault was a terrible thing. It was home to all the nasty things people had done to me. All the nasty things we all do to each other without thinking, just acting. Even friends had places in my vault. If someone said something mean, it went in the vault. if a family member said something mean, it went in the vault. I never let one single thing go. Never. If you left me waiting for you somewhere and you weren't on time, in the vault it went.

I would bring out the bad memories when they were needed. So if, say, someone asked me for a favour at anytime, Bang! Into the vault, to remember the last time they screwed me. And then I would do that favour anyway – but not before I looked through the vault. The vault stopped me from having fun. It kept me locked in the past, never able to forgive anyone for anything.

If we were invited to a party at a friend's house, say, and the last time I was hanging out with them something happened that made me uncomfortable at that time, into the vault it would go. If the thing was bad enough, then I would worry all week about whether it was going to happen again. I would think, what did I do for this bad thing to happen? Then every morning I would run with that in my head. How could this person do this to me? How can I make it right? I have to make it right! Or I might do the opposite and just use the vault to get out of things and say to my wife, remember what happened last time with them? I am not going there because I hate them now.

Do you get the vault? It is hate stored up and ready to be unleashed at any time. What kind of life was I living, just holding on to so much hate and turning it inward all the time?

The vault had to go. As much as I loved the vault because it protected me from being hurt over and over again by people, it also stopped me from living. It stopped me from forgiving and experiencing new things and having fun. Imagine having fun, that whole self-love thing. To forgive is divine. I never thought that was true.

So I walked into therapy and I took a deep breath and I talked about the vault....

Burying the vault.

I told my therapist about the vault and how evil it was and how bad of a person I was for having this horrible thing and she just smiled and asked me what I would like to do with the vault. I said I would love to bury it and forget about everything in it and never ever go into it again. She calmly said to me let's bury it then....

So we started she asked me where I wanted to do it and I told her, my back yard. She asked me what I saw and what I smelled and what I wanted to feel with my hands. We covered all five senses so I could completely go there in my mind.

I closed my eyes and took deep breaths and she talked to me and used my information to transport me to my back yard with my pond running and me sitting on my back porch. She asked me what the vault looked like and how big it was. I told her it was an old, rusty, red vault with a swinging door and a handle that locked the vault. It was 4 feet tall and 4 feet deep. It was beside me on my back porch and so was my poor dog Moe, whom I had recently put to sleep. He was there with me to give me strength for what seemed to be an impossible task.

I bear-hugged this vault and carried it to the front of my shed. I placed it down nice and gently and walked away. My hands were covered with rust from the carrying the vault. I could smell the metal on my hands. (The more real you make it with your senses the better it is to do this type of therapy.)

I got my shovel and began to dig a deep hole, my beautiful dog just sitting and watching me as I dug the new home for this god-forsaken vault I created so long ago I could not even remember. Once the hole was big enough to fit the vault, the therapist asked me to take a moment and think about all the worry I had and fold each worry like I was folding freshly-washed laundry and make it real neat and give each item as much time as I would like to then take each worry and place it in the vault.

Next take all the bad things I had stored about family and friends and people in general and do the same: be nice and kind to these things and fold them up as neatly as I can, place them in the vault, and then close that door. I have given too much time to all these things and now I can say goodbye to them.

So I put this heavy vault, this rusty old hate- and worry-filled thing in the hole, nice and gently and then I walked past my best friend Moe and got my shovel and I filled that hole with dirt and I walked away and sat back on my back porch and Moe sat beside me and I cried and I showed emotion for the first time at therapy and now I knew that I was capable of actually changing and working through this. The vault was buried and I really had no reason to dig it up or go back there. All the stuff in the rusty old thing wasn't worth my time. Now I could start living and start learning to be myself.

This is the actual thought record I had after that session were we buried the vault.

Thought record::::::

Burying the vault...

Sit::::

I buried the vault and I don't need to look at it or dig it up or watch over it with my dog...

Mood:::::

Depressed 80% Anxious 80% Trapped and Ashamed 80%

Thoughts:::::

I need to watch over the vault.

No don't there is nothing but pain and heart ache there I don't need to go back there.

I brought my dog with me and I feel guilty for having him there.

I love Moe I miss him and he kept me company while I was there I need to let go of the guilt I have for putting him down. I need for the both of us to walk out of my back yard and leave those worries and bad things behind now. I have given them too much. I have given them too many tears and I have to stop now and not look back.

I need to leave this place behind. It's dark and scary and I don't belong there with those bad things I'm not a bad person.

Thought record:

Going to have a good day

Moods:

Nervous 100%, Anxious 90%

Situation:

I'm going to take it easy today. I'm going to take deep breaths. I'm going to think about my hot thoughts. I'm going to write them down. I'm going to use balanced thinking. I'm going to fight and fight and fight today. Not going to let it grab me or come near me today. I will not spiral down. I'm going to be strong!!!

Thoughts:

I'm having a good day I have done very well fighting off my depression. It has not grabbed me once today!!

Today was a wicked day. I stayed happy and strong and never let it grab me........ and played my bass again, which was great. I'm fighting the good fight!!! I am learning everyday

Guilt

I had so much guilt that when I went to therapy to talk about it I didn't know where to start. I felt guilty for so many things, things I am not at fault for at all. I am working at getting over this guilt, by proving to myself that those feelings are wrong.

When I was on vacation I thought that I could go without writing things down and try to just live this new life I have and enjoy learning to be me. But it lasted three days before I started to spiral, thinking about these things I am guilty of. These feelings consumed me, till I started to write and beat these guilty thoughts. Whenever I start feeling guilty now I know I have to write it down and attack these guilty thoughts with balanced thinking. The key is I now recognize the spiral when it starts and I write it down prove it wrong.

There are things I feel guilty for.

When I was 22, I started having health problems and I went to a specialist about it and soon after I found out that I was sterile. The guilt I had for not being able to have children was huge and it ate me up every day. At one point I even apologized to my father for being sterile and not being able to have children. The guilt was over whelming. I had a surgery to try to fix this but it was unsuccessful. Following that I went for more and more tests and two more operations. I found out that I have a mutated gene of Cystic Fibrosis. That gene is very rare and strange. The condition it caused added up to months of tests and humiliation.

I felt so guilty for this and I had no choice in the matter. I felt that I was disappointing my wife and family by not being able to have children. We then tried artificial insemination and that was even worse. We did not get pregnant and we spent a lot of money trying. I saw myself as the cause of all this, of six years of pure guilt and self-hatred.

I had to reason it out I had to prove yourself wrong. and move on.

Thought record:

Being sterile

Sit:

After several operations and years of tests I am sterile.

Moods:

Guilty 100%, Humiliated 100%

Thoughts:

I cannot have children. I am a failure. I have disappointed my wife and family.

How is it that I am a failure? This is a medical condition. I had no choice in the matter. I tried and went through years of testing and several operations. I should not feel bad for anything. I did not ask for any of this to happen.

My poor wife deserves more from life – to be pregnant and to have children. I have robbed her of all this joy.

My wife loves me and has stuck with me through all this. She is my biggest fan and I love her with all my heart. This difficulty makes us stronger and stronger. Our life together is filled with so much and we did it all together.

How can I just keep living and being such a failure?

I am not a failure. Feeling guilty for this is just wrong. None of what happened is my fault and now I have to forgive myself and stop feeling guilty. I have to realize that bad things happen and life is very often challenging for people. I can't change everything and I am not responsible for everything that happens in life.

I need to relax and just let it go. We have a beautiful son, and we are happy. Sterility was just a bump in the road and nothing else. Life is moving on and that chapter is over. Feeling guilty about it and not moving on is silly. I am wasting time carrying this guilt.

I can forgive people for things they have done to me and things that they have said about me. I have to forgive myself and love myself. After all I am the most important person in my life and giving myself a break is the right thing to do. Forgiveness is a great gift. It is mine to give. I forgive myself for this. My wife loves me. I have a son. No more guilt for being sterile. It is gone I am free...

Debt. I feel such guilt over money and how it has been wasted. I feel that I have failed so badly as a person by having debt. I have lain in bed many nights, wasting hours not sleeping but feeling guilty about the debt we have. How humiliating it is even writing this out right now, but the money is gone and now it is replaced by guilt. And humiliation and worries. I don't remember buying all this with my line of credit.

Just because we used this money for day care and home improvements and other things doesn't make me a bad person. Nor should I feel shame for it. I will not go to hell. I will not be shunned when I walk down the street. Perhaps people reading this right now will find what I am saying to be shocking, but I don't care. Here is the thing.

Thought record:

Debt

Sit:

We have debt

Moods:

Guilt 100%, Humiliation 100%

Thoughts:

We have used up our line of credit. How will I ever pay it back, I am such a loser and I should be ashamed of myself.

It is only money.When I pay off my house I will start paying down the line of credit, and my house is paid for in three years. Debt does not make me a bad person. My wife loves me. I have friends and my son loves me. Just because I may not have cash to spare at the end of the month because of an extra payment doesn't mean I am a bad person.

I should have never got this line of credit to begin with.

I got it and used it for new windows in the basement and many other things. It has helped us out a lot and it will again as I pay it down. I am a responsible person and I always pay every month, so what is the big deal here? There is really no reason that we should not have used our line of credit.

What if I can't make a payment? will they take my house?

No they will not take my house. I have missed a payment before and I called and they just took the payment the week after. There is no problem here at all.

I need to just realize that this guilt is ridiculous and that I can't change the past. What has happened has happened and owing money is the way life is. This doesn't make me a bad person. It makes me human and that's what I am. There is no fiery hell for people who owe money or have huge credit card debt. That place would be full of people if that was the case.

Feeling guilt over numbers in a bank account is stupid and I know that I am not stupid. I know that I am not a bad person, so that guilt is gone. I will fight to keep that way, just like I fight so much else off and sooner or later it will be gone permanently.

I forgive myself for spending money fruitlessly. I am human and humans do things that don't make sense, because we are human.

Thought record:

My dog.

Sit:

I killed my dog!

Mood:

Guilty80%, Sad 80%

Thought:

I killed my dog.

He was sick and was only going to get worse. I did the right thing!

Why wouldn't he just die on his own?

I asked him and told him he could go and he deserved it. He was a good dog. He always made me happy. I told him I loved him and I held him while he died.

I'll never see him again.

No one knows that and no one can say that I may never see him again. He lives in my heart and I'll never let him go....

Moe —The guilt I have for putting my dog to sleep is so great at times that I am brought to tears. Moe was my dog. I brought him home from the pound. He was my best friend. There are no words I can write or say that could come close to expressing how I feel about him. Anyone who has a pet knows what I am talking about.

Moe was old. The time I spent with him flew by too fast. Fourteen years gone in the blink of an eye. Moe got old and he lost a lot of weight and he was sick. Sometimes he couldn`t stand up on his own and I had to lift him up so he could go outside. Sometimes he would fall over as well. His health was bad. I admit it now. I had to put him to sleep. Many times at bed time he would lie in his bed and I would get down on the floor and I would lie with him and he would rest his head on my arm and I would look him in the eyes and tell him it was okay for him to go. I told him many times that I loved him and that he was a good boy and he always made me happy. I would kiss him on the nose and we would lie there, just looking at each other till he fell asleep. He stayed with me till the end. I think he didn't want to die alone. I had to put him down. The day I did, he lay between my legs and rested his chin on my lap the way he had done a thousand times since I brought him home. Once again I looked him in the eye and told him the same thing: I loved him. He was a good boy and he always made me happy.

This guilt I cannot beat haunts me every day. I fight it all the time. I reason it out. I know I did the right thing. He was sick and I know that it was the best thing to do and I know he is free from pain and I know all these things to be 100% true. But the guilt is still there. Sometimes for days in a row, and sometimes not. But I believe that sooner or later I will forgive myself for Moe's death, and I will only have good memories of my best friend Moe.

Guilt is powerful but forgiveness is so much stronger. Being able to forgive someone in your life is so fulfilling. But being able to forgive yourself is so empowering and up lifting. To be able to just forgive yourself and move on should be the easiest thing of all. You are human. You make mistakes. Move on and stop the guilt. Forgive yourself.

Learning to be human...

Learning to be human what does that mean?? We are all human. We all breathe. We all bleed when cut. We all feel and react to our environments. So that makes us all human. But to be human is to make mistakes and to learn from those mistakes. I want to talk about how I learned to be human.

Making mistakes:

We all make mistakes in life – small ones or big ones, they're all the same. Learning that it's okay to make mistakes was a huge task for me. I always tried to do everything right. The right way was my way. no other way was acceptable.

So, say my wife has the day off. She works hard all week so she enjoys her day off. Then the house is messy and I come home. I realize that she has done nothing all day. Before, I would think, that was a big mistake. She wasted her day completely and I would be so pissed off I would tell her, "How could you be so lazy? It's not fair that I work on my day off and clean the house and do the gardening and so on and so on." But now I know that she made no mistake at all. I made the mistake in thinking I could control her on her day off. I had to stop thinking I could control her. I needed to change my way of thinking. I needed to acknowledge my mistakes and then let them go completely and just leave it at that.

So I started. I did something totally out of my comfort zone. I took Sunday off!!!

I did nothing on Sunday except play with my son and play my bass and I do no house work and I just have a day off. Holy Smokes! I am bent out of shape over it all day. I think, what a mistake, not doing this work and not using my free time wisely. What a jackass, just sitting around playing Uno with my son. Swimming and walking to the park and just relaxing – what a dummy!

But over time, I got used to it. Today I took a day off work and I am writing this sitting in a chair in front of a coffee shop and not gardening or cleaning the house. Is that a mistake? No! The gardening can wait. The dirty floors can wait. Even if it was a mistake, it doesn't matter - there are no consequences to my taking a day off to enjoy myself. No-one is going to fire me from my job as me. There is no overlord saying, "You did nothing on your day off! You will rot in hell."

It's the same with all mistakes big and small.

I do all the shipping and receiving at work so I have all these invoices and packing slips and a computer to input all the stuff that comes into the store. It's a big job. I fix and setup guitars and amps as well. I sell things and I am the assistant manager at the store. I work very hard.

I would get emails from head office about something that wasn't received into the computer. I used to freak out and think, "I am such a loser. I can't do anything right." Then I would have to fix the problem and email back that I fixed it. And they would email me back and thank me. This caused me great stress and I hated it when I had to fix things. It was humiliating to me that I messed up at all. But then I changed my way of thinking: I wasn't screwing up at all. I was being human.

Before that point, I was fixing mistakes but I wasn't moving on. They would email me back and say thank you but I would just stay in the depressed mood humiliated for my mistake not able to move on and I would let it consume me the whole day thoughts of failure. All I did was miscount how many guitar straps there were in a pile of maybe 100, while also setting up a guitar and helping a salesman with a question about financing a sale. I might have been doing 3 things at once. *Let it go.* Fix it and move on. No one is going to fire me over a guitar strap. Again, there is no overlord watching me count inventory. I am not dammed to hell over miscounted straps. I made a mistake. *Move on.* I would get three emails a month about missing things. It just happens because I am human and I will make a mistake.

So I started being nice to these strangers sending me these emails. I would say, "Sorry. My bad." with a smiley face and they would mail back and say no problem and smiley face back. Sometimes if it was a big item that was missing and never shipped I would call these ladies at head office and talk to them and they were nice. They were human, like me. They never fired me and never got angry with me. It was a guitar that was missing. "We'll find it," she would say. How about that?? Being human was nice!!

The world is never going to end over a mistake. If I do work on someone's guitar and they don't like the way it plays, that's okay. I will fix it while they wait and make sure they like it. I won't spiral down anymore and think what a waste I am, I must be the worst guitar repairman ever, just because of this one guy who prefers his guitar to play a certain way. I just let it go.

If an amplifier comes in and while I am working on it it happens to blow up because of a mistake I made in wiring I don`t lose sleep over it anymore. The world didn`t end and the guy whose amp it is won`t come and kill me while I sleep. I will call him and tell him his amp needs to be shipped out to be fixed and I will supply him with another amp while he waits for his to be fixed. Mistakes happen and there really is no way around that. We are human and like it or not humans make mistakes. Learn from those mistakes and move on. Don`t hold on to them and keep them locked in a vault like I did. Never treat any friends different for making mistakes or even family because one wrong thing or one wrong action doesn`t make someone a bad person. They just made a mistake and that's it. They're still your friend they're still your brother or sister and they would never hold a mistake against you. And if they did, you would say to them, "I made a mistake. I am sorry. Will you forgive me?" And you need to learn to forgive because being human is about making mistakes and about learning to forgive people.

Just remember this saying, ``to err is human, to forgive divine." I never really believed it till now.

This is a powerful thought record about my Mom and Dad. Being human is so hard.

Thought record:

I am spiraling fast...

Sit:

My Mom and Dad move into a retirement home....

Mood:

Sad 100%, Anxiety 100%, Depressed 100%, Overwhelmed 100%

Thoughts:

Is it the right thing for them to go into a retirement home?

Yes they are both deteriorating in health and will be looked after and fed and they will not have to worry about all the things they have been worrying about.

I feel empty. I feel empty because it is a step closer to them dying. This is one of the starting points to saying goodbye. Now I know I may only have a small number of years left with them.

I always thought they would be there forever. Now my super hero dad is mortal after all. The man I have looked up to all my life is crippled and walks with a walker. He can no longer make meals and has a hard time holding a glass in his hand to drink from. It is destroying me. He is all I ever wanted to be as a father and he is whom I think of when I raise my son. His work ethic is ingrained deep into me.He worked his ass off and his hands are crippled from years of work. He deserves what he is getting. He gave all he had raising seven boys and now he gets to rest and he gets to be looked after, much like both he and my mother did for us all our lives.

Maybe I need to let them be human and let them relax and not look at them the same way and love them for who they are and accept that they are old and need help. They are human. My father is flesh and bone, not Superman. As much as

I loved him as a superhero, I love him even more now, seeing how much he has suffered for all of us his whole life.

It is over whelming. I am overcome with emotions, good and bad, the past two days. I don't know how to deal with it. I am new to this whole thing of actually feeling and recognizing all this emotion. I am still learning how to act human and react to all that is happening. This week has been so powerful and challenging for me, but I am still here. I am still right here, learning and rolling with the punches.

"Nothing worth having doesn't come without some kind of fight... you gotta kick at the darkness till it bleeds daylight"

I'm learning that it's okay to be a human. But it's so hard.

I am so driven to get better that I did a test. The following is my test to see just what would happen if I just enjoyed myself for a change and had to do nothing!

Stopping worry

When I started running it wasn't easy at all. Just being able to run for 60 seconds was a huge task. It took a very long time for me to work up to being able to run for five minutes without stopping. Learning to control my breathing and my pace and building up the muscles in my body was a huge task. When I was in college I would spend hours playing scales in every key building my knowledge of my basses fret board and my speed and rhythm, my dexterity so I was able to use the scales and improvise walking bass lines over chord changes flawlessly.

The need to control your breathing while running holds many people back. Some people think that you have to take fast shallow breaths and not just relax and breathe normally. Many people will take a deep breath and hold it while they are running, but the key is to breathe normally, like you always do – just nice and relaxed and without effort.

Before you know it, with repetition and practice and a lot of time, your breathing just happens and you don't even think about it at all.

I worried a lot about everything work money, upcoming gigs, you name it. I used to check my bank account five times a day, always checking to see how much money was there and how broke we were and the bills I had to pay. It would snowball: the more I checked the worse I felt about myself and what

I had to do to get out of debt. It was just a bad scene altogether. Worry was a major thing with my depression. It made me work harder and it made me a nervous wreck at times. I worried all the time. I had to learn that I could live life without worry. I buried the vault and I wasn't going to dig it up, so now I had to work on not worrying, just like I worked on my breathing when I was learning to run and my scales and modes when I was in college was learning about music.

So I read a book called *Escaping Emotional Entrapment*. It's the best book I ever read. I learned so much from this book.

Here is the thing: there is only one thing we have to do and that is die! I recognized that this worry was caused by looking at my bank account all day and hating myself so much for not making enough money. So I stopped doing it every day. I couldn't just totally leave it and never look so I cut it down to once a day and that greatly decreased my stress. I did that for one month, then I cut a day out and then two days, then three days and then four days and I took weekends off. Now I am down to two days a month, my pay day and the next Monday of following week.

I also stopped looking at my bills every day. I don't need to keep looking at them. They're not going anywhere. They're on my desk. Just paying them is enough and if I am late, I am late. There is no need for me to worry about a bill. It's a piece of paper on my desk... I will pay the bills when I get paid, like I always have.

I was starting to learn to control worry. I was learning I can control my own emotions and that nothing in life has to happen. I don't have to do anything but die! And I was learning that I really didn't want to die at all.

I have left bills for so long that I have gotten shut off notices and I have called the hydro company and water company and had such nice phone conversations with the people on the other line. I use my business voice I use at work and I tell them they're just going to have to wait till I get paid.

Guess what – the world didn't end. I am not dead and my service never got cut off, and they got their money in the end.

What if I didn't pay them in time!!! Oh my God – would I have been a horrible person? Would all my friends and family look at me differently? Would I spiral down and want to kill myself? Not anymore! None of these thoughts entered my mind. For the first time ever I was learning not to worry. I am not going to say I never worry or I never have these thoughts, because I do, but I fight them tooth and nail and I do thought records to prove nothing catastrophic is going to happen if I stop worrying...

Worry raises blood pressure. It creates anxiety. It causes fights with your wife or husband. It kills self-esteem and causes you not to sleep. But I've got news for you: it does nothing to help any situation. So you can pick your major worry and slowly get rid of it. Prove it wrong with thought records and once you tackle the big one then the other worries will just not bother you anymore.

Here are thought records from when I was trying to beat worry.

Thought record:

What if???

Sit:

What if I stopped worrying about things I can't control and stopped caring so much about everything I do for just one day!!!!

Mood:

Anxious 80%, Excited 90%, Fearful 80%.

Thoughts:

I could just work at a normal pace. The work will get done, maybe not today but it will get done!

I won't be over stressed and spiral down!!

I will feel good about not getting depressed..

The world will still CARRY on if I take it easy and don't stress.

Maybe my boss will see that I actually need help if I don't break my back to get everything done in one day.

I am sick of the way I am and I need to change and I am working hard at learning how to not spiral.

I think that I deserve to not be depressed anymore!

One day won't hurt anyone and who knows maybe if it goes well I'll do it. Tomorrow as well.

Journal entry:

Whenever I worry about shit nothing happens. I waste all this time losing sleep and age myself for no reason at all. I worried about a gig and inventory for a week. I lost sleep, for what?? Nothing at all. It all went off without a hitch. No problem. When will I learn worry is a waste of time?

Thought record:

First Monday of the New Year.

Sit::

I feel anxious and hopeless. I am just overwhelmed today. I feel like I just want to disappear again. Haven't felt like this in a long, long time. My office is filled with 30 guitars and 5 guitar amp's to be repaired and people are calling wondering why there stuff isn't fixed. The store hasn't calmed down after the Christmas rush I am short staffed and I can't leave the sales floor. There is one repair that has me worried the most. A old Martin acoustic I made a pick guard for.

Mood:

Anxious 80%, Trapped 70%, Hopeless 60%.

Thoughts:

I am anxious about a repair I did to a guitar on Friday. I hand-made a pick guard and put it on a very expensive martin guitar. I am very self-critical about my work and I feel the customer will not be happy with it and may cause a scene and not want to pay for it.

I did my best and if he doesn't like it then I will not charge him and that is all I can do. I did my best and that's all I can do. I had never done that repair before.

l feel trapped. I didn't sleep last night and I had so much running through my head and I can't shut down my bad thoughts. Once I start, I can't stop.

I am trying. I couldn't shut down. That happens and I need to stop bringing my work home with me. I need to accept the fact that I can't change things by worrying about them all the time. I have to stop worrying about stuff I can't change.

So dude came and got his guitar I made the pick guard for and he loved it so all the worrying and lack of sleep was for nothing.

I pull myself out of that mood by 12:00 today, 6 hours faster than normal. Bring on the day

Breaking all my rules

Six days off from work and I am going to have fun. I am not going to do things I would normally feel I have to do. This is going to be very stressful, but at the same time it will be fun proving that I don't really have to do anything!!!

Thursday – Day 1:

I got up at 5:00. I was planning on running a half-marathon, 21km, but instead I just worked on my book and actually played my bass for fun for once. Then I was planning on doing my gardening because all my plants and vines are out of control. I would have started at 7:00 am worked straight though till I was finished. Time would have been spent on self-hate and worrying about money and stuff like that. But not today!!

I decided to go for a 5 km run instead, so I got ready and my wife looked at me and said, "Are you getting back now or are you leaving?" I said, "I am leaving." She smiled and said, "Have fun!!" I was blown away. So I left and I had a fun run. Now I enjoy my time alone. I smile while I run. Then I got home and I walked my son to school. Then, instead of going home and working in the yard I walked to the coffee shop and I sat there and worked on this book for an hour. No gardening!! Then I went to work. Why? To talk to my friend Nelson and get the store's whippersnipper. That's right. I am going to take the stores whippersnipper and use it till I feel like bringing it back!!And I don't care! The world is not going to end. I am not going to get fired. I am going to whipper-snip.

So I got home and I made myself a nice coffee and went downstairs and got one of my basses – my G&L, which I have had since I was 19 – and I sat and played it. No scales. No tunes to work on I just played and had fun. It was nice. It was a long time since I had fun playing my bass. I played for 2 hours!! I enjoyed myself and nothing happened but that fun. I ate a small lunch, then I gardened and I didn't think about bills or money or anything. All I did was pay attention to what I was doing, pulling weeds, cutting vines cleaning up, making it the way I like my garden to look. I got lost in the moment. Not once did I think anything bad about myself. I just worked and enjoyed the quiet of my back yard and the beautiful flowers I have worked hard to keep happy all these years.

I love my back yard it is a little get-away from the rest of the world. I never thought that before, but it is and I love it. I whippersnipped and finished the back yard. I was supposed to do the front yard as well but it can wait. I have 5 more days of time off. It's too funny. I just would have never ever said something like that.

I cleaned up and had a nice cold glass of sangria (wine with orange juice and lime-ade). I sat in the sun and closed my eyes and went to my safe place, my tree. I love my safe place! I went to my tree as a reward today for the hard work I had done. I closed my eyes and I breathed in through my leaves and out through my roots I took the time to just think of being the tree to relax and center myself. This was a new trip to the tree for me something new I was not going there because I needed to get away from anything there was no trigger no spiral to stop! I was going there to just relax this was such a pleasure meditating for the first time just taking joy in being alive and enjoying this moment in the tree breathing deep in through my leaves and out though my roots just doing that letting the world melt away and nothing else mattered but my happiness and me being this tree. It was incredible if being human met actually feeling like this then this is something I am going to do more often. I stayed in the tree for a long time till I was happy and content loving the moment.

I then stepped out of the tree and finished my drink walked to school and picked up my son. I started the barbeque and I made dinner with a nice salad and when Sherri came home I had dinner on the table. We went swimming. A friend of Sherri's came over and we hung out together. What a nice day and I broke so many rules that day. I felt so good doing it. The world didn't end. I didn't get fired for taking the whippersnipper. I may never bring it back, ha! I had a great day...

Friday – Day 2:

Friday morning, again I let my alarm go off and I slept in. I didn't run my half-marathon I got up at 7:00 and ran another relaxing, fun, in-the-moment 5 km. I dropped my son off at school and came home and had coffee with my wife. She left for an appointment and I told her to walk downtown and I'll meet her there and we'll make a day of it just hanging out downtown before we pick up our son at 3:00. Doing that is so out of my comfort zone it's not funny. Still, no half marathon and the front yard gardens are a total mess and now I have arranged it so I'll get no work done at all. But I will have a good time hanging out with my wife.

I met Sherri right on time. We got coffee and sat under a tree in a small park by the library and just talked and watched birds. There were a couple of dirty, homeless dudes smelling up the park but it didn't matter. We just laughed and talked and I said I feel like a high school kid skipping class and hanging with his girlfriend. It made Sherri very happy. Just a couple of high school kids hanging out, up to no good. We sat there for an hour, under that tree, and it seemed like 20 minutes. Time flew by. I didn't worry about a thing, not anything. No bills, no self-hate for not doing yard work, no guilt for not running the half marathon. Just peace and love and laughing. It was great.

We then got lunch and walked to another park and ate and watched small children with their parents, playing on a playground. It brought back memories for us of our own son playing in the same park. We walked home and Sherri vacuumed the pool and I packed my bass amp and stuff for my gig that night and played my bass for a while. Our neighbor Josie came over and swam in the pool with us till I had to pick Dylan up. What a day. Dylan came home and I played in the pool with him till I had to leave for my gig.

The gig was packed we played on a patio and I hated it. I am having a hard time playing music now. It triggers me like crazy, triggers my self-hate and worry and humiliation. If I drink a few beers the triggers are worse. I really think it is time for me to stop playing music. I think I need a break. I have been playing professionally since I was 14 and I have never gone more than one week without a gig. That is very impressive: I have always been in demand and people seek me out to play with them. But I truly feel I need to stop. Years and years of triggering depression at every gig has taken its toll on me and this gig was no exception. It is really bad when the only reason I now put a bass on is to make money. That is it. No fun and no passion at all. I need to take a step back and maybe try to remember why I even started playing in the first place.

The second day ended on a bad note but I dug myself out once I was home. I sat in the dark on my patio and went to my safe place and let the outside world disappear around me. I opened my eyes and went to bed. My wife rolled over and thanked me for the most wonderful day she has had in a long time. She told me she is so in love with me and how proud she is of me. Do you know what I did!! Kissed her on the lips and I told her I loved as well and then I said thank you. I accepted her complement!!! That was that. I went to sleep. No worry about anything that didn't get done or any self-hate about the gig and the many triggers from it. Just peace and love and sleep. What a day. Ups and downs, but more ups than downs. I am still here, just smiling as I drift off to sleep

Saturday – Day 3:

Slept in and snuggled with my son. Watched Saturday morning cartoons. Sherri left for her work-out class. I had a coffee on my back porch and just relaxed. Then I worked in my front yard. I had cut back all the beautiful lavender bushes. Before that, they were huge and they all died from the long, hard winter we had. As I cut them back and I thought about every cut I made. Each one was like me cutting back everything from my past and learning to let it go and make way for new growth, new life for the lavender and for me at the same time. It may take years for the lavender to grow as big as it was but I don't care. I just let it grow and the same with me. I am learning so much. Sometimes I have good days and sometimes bad but I am getting there day by day, moment by moment. I spent two hours out front working and enjoyed it all. Never a bad thought and never a thought about work, which normally by that point in the day would have got into my head. I would have called at least three times by now worried about inventory or something like that thinking that if I am not at work or having contact with work that something bad will happen. But I am learning to not take work home with me that the work is not going anywhere and it will be there when I get back. Me worrying and calling is not going to change anything at the store. Learning to let go of things and not worry is turning out to be a very good thing. Something I have to let grow as well.

Sherri came home and we visited my mom and dad. That was when my day took a down turn. I love my mom and dad so much and they are having a hard time. They are old, in their 80's and just moved into a retirement home. Dad is having a hard time walking, which is hard enough, but Sherri gets on his case for not using his walker. By the time we leave I am a complete mess, almost crying while I am driving and I can't even breathe. We fight in the car. Sherri has a bad temper and she says she never wants' to go there again because all they do is bitch and she just goes on and on... Everyone is treating my mom and dad like they don't have any choices in life anymore and treating them like they're not even human. I am destroyed by this whole thing. By the time I get home I am just a mess and I talk with Sherri and I tell her how I feel and I cry... I actually show emotion and tell her what's on my mind. I don't stash anything in the vault. The vault is gone, buried, not there anymore. I talk about my feelings.

The phone rings and I am just a mess and Sherri's brothers are coming over with their kids for a pool party I am still just in the middle of a breakdown, so I go for a run. It was 90 degrees out. I got my stuff on and Sherri says she is sorry. I leave on my run and I take a different way than usual. I run along the 12 mile creek and I just relax and think look at the trees and the forest and the raging river. I take in the smells and the birds flying in the bushes as I run down the path. It is all so beautiful and peaceful. I remember my father when he was young and throwing the baseball in the back yard with me after dinner in the shade of the trees in our back yard. His throw was so hard it hurt my hand sometimes. He would smile and say, "Throw it hard. Aim for my face. That way you know it will be a good throw." We would throw that ball for an hour. Sometimes we would talk while we played and other times not a word was said.

I remembered how after a while a friend would come over and I would ditch my dad and leave to play with my friend. And I would feel bad. One time I was riding my bike down the street with my friend Mark and I said I am going home and I went back to play with my dad instead. My dad is my hero. He is the one I look up to. He is everything I wish I could be in a father. And now he is old. And I still love him and he is still who I want to be when I grow up.

Before I knew it I was done my 5 km run and I walked home. While I walked home I went to my safe place, my tree. I stayed there and regrouped for just a short time before I got home to a pool party with screaming little 6 year olds. At the end of the day, after it was all over, Sherri said she was so sorry for her actions and that she loves me and she was so happy I actually talked to her about what was in my head. I smiled to myself and though what a rough day, but I made it through. I used the tools I have been given. Thank you, Mastora. I went to my safe place. I am learning to be myself here, ladies and gentlemen, slowly but surely. My dream will come true.

Sunday – Day 4:

To forgive is divine. Today my brother-in-law came over with his 2 sons for a pool party. Without Sherri there it was a big step for me. My brother-in-law was once one of my best friends. I hung out with him all the time. He started smoking some bad stuff. He would disappear for days at a time. We would hunt for him and find him and I pulled him out of 2 crack houses. I would finish a gig and then drive back to St Catharines and search till 5 am sometimes for him. He lost everything, his house, his girlfriend. Let's say that our relationship has not really existed for at least 10 years. In that time he has had two little boys whom we all have had turns looking after while he struggled through life. Now he is getting his shit back together. I have harbored so much hate for him and at the same time missed the guy he used to be. Today I took a large step and let him in to my life and had him over by myself. He brought coffees and the boys played and we just talked and watched.

I am ready to forgive him for all he has done to me, to his sister (my wife), and the rest of his family. Maybe just having him in my life again will help him as well. The time of hating is over and gone. The vault is gone, so I have to open my heart and just forgive him. The boys played and played and swam and swam. Sherri came home and was blown away that he was over with the boys. Her face lit up when she looked at me because I normally wouldn't have been in the same room as this man if I didn't have to be. The day just flew by and before we knew it they were leaving.

We went out to dinner with a friend and his wife, then to see a band play and no sooner did we get there than this friend of mine made a comment about my intelligence and I shut it out and it rolled off my back. I feel like a Jedi knight sometimes now, like I have these powers and no one knows it. So when they try to hurt me like they used to by making fun of me and laughing at me it does nothing. I acknowledge the trigger, I prove it wrong, and it is powerless. And then I wonder why I have these people as friends, why I go out with them and why I bother to even waste time with them.

The rest of the night was fun. The bass player in the band was just horrible and it was funny after the first set the drummer came over and introduced the band to us and the bass player looked at me and said everybody knows who Darcy Patrick is. That brought a smile to my face and I looked over at my son and he was smiling ear to ear it was flattering I took the complement and left it at that. I introduced my wife and son to the bass player.

We went home that night and had a drink on the back porch and talked for a while then went to bed. This week of breaking the rules is proving to be a good lesson for me. Using my tools every day to beat depression is turning out to be fun and maybe rebuilding my friendship with my brother-in-law will be a good thing. Acknowledging triggers and dealing with them may prove that I am not in need of some people as friends in the end and that`s okay. Sometimes, friends just grow apart. It`s not my job to fix or make people like me anymore!! Day 4 was a good day!!!

Monday – Day 5:

Monday was a no communication from anyone day. I turned off my phone and never contacted a single person. Not even the friend I went out with for dinner last night, who tried to make fun of me by insulting my intelligence and making me a joke. Normally I would have contacted him and tried to communicate and make things right by bending and kissing ass to make myself feel better.

But I didn't do that, and I won't ever again. That is not me anymore. Happiness comes from within, not from other people. I never even checked my work email today, either, and I know there will be emails asking me where shipments are and is my guitar ready and some stuff my boss wants done. But I never checked and they can all wait till Wednesday, when I get back to work.

Usually I would have checked every day and called the store once a day to make sure things were going well but not today. Not this week, not anymore. I am breaking all my rules and working on using all my tools. These 6 days off have changed the way I live my life forever. Everything I have learned I am putting to use and it is all working and it is making me feel strong and happy. I feel so damn good I'm looking forward to getting back to work on Wednesday and applying these tools there. But that's another day away.

I played with my son all day today. We swam for a long time, then played Uno. We walked to the store and he used some money from his piggy bank to buy Lego and we played with it. It was a good lesson in play today: mindless fun, bonding, laughing, loving life, and living in the moment. Just playing nothing else mattered except fun, with no contact from the outer world at all.

I made dinner for the three of us had it ready on the table when Sherri got home. I did the dishes and swam some more, then finished the night off with *Star Wars: Return of the Jedi*, and off to bed. Just a fun day of getting lost in play living in the moment and getting pure joy out of simply things. Life really could never get any better than today.

Tuesday – Day 6:

Today I ran a 10 km run and felt really good. I enjoyed my run and had nothing but good thoughts the whole time. Work starts tomorrow and it was on my mind today. I have to be honest: I did worry about it for some time. I thought about all the work I will have to do to make the store functional and clean up all the mess that will be there when I get back with the shipping and receiving. I know that I don't have to do it all in one day and I know that I have tools to deal with what is going to happen tomorrow, but it still doesn't make it easy going back there after 6 days off. I will take deep breaths and use my new tools to not spiral and I will not spiral...

Today I also made dinner for the whole gang at the pool and I am realizing that I like to cook. I think I have made dinner, breakfast, lunch every day since I have been off. I enjoy cooking and cleaning. I also played my bass today for a long time, three hours. I am trying to remember why I started playing, because I am concerned that I might have to stop playing. Music is a powerful trigger for me. I have been playing for so long I need to try to remember why I started. It seems I only play for money now and I never enjoy myself anymore when I play. I am speechless when it comes to music. It has meant so much to me and now I just spiral at gigs and end up in a dark place. It is truly disturbing me and that is not good.

These six days:

These six days were very exciting and very happy days. I worked through a lot of stuff and I feel that I have accomplished a lot in the way of beating worry, and beating the have to's and supposed to's and learning that there really isn't any consequences to pay if I don't do something the way I feel I have to or need to. I also played a lot and got lost in the moment and took joy from doing small things. I did gardening and I enjoyed it. It wasn't a self-hate fest. These six days were an experiment gone right. I succeeded at enjoying myself. I feel proud and happy. All these things are new and exciting to me. It was a good mini-vacation!!

Where I work is not who I am

I used to work for a family run music store. I had been dealing with this store for so long that I can't even remember a time when I didn't shop there. I learned how to run a music store through a high school co-op in this store. I learned how to fix guitars and amps, as well as ordering, shipping, receiving, and merchandizing. I taught there for several years as well as working part time for cash, under the table at first.

I was hired part time and was put on the payroll. To say that I loved my worked is to say the truth. To say I loved were I worked would have been a lie. Because in fact this place was just an extension of high school and grade school. The people I worked with abused me every day. They made fun of my weight and I played along to make them laugh because that was who I was at the time. My goal was make people like me. Being the brunt of all these jokes and having everyone laugh at me was easy to accept. Part time work turned to full time work and that meant more hours and more humiliation. I was learning so much as far as business goes and we grew as a store and I got all my musician friends jobs. To this day the store is staffed with my friends. But every day was a humiliation fest. I withdrew into myself and played the game. I made people laugh and I was the brunt of all the jokes from my friends, even the ones I had actually got jobs for at the store.

One day a very terrifying thing happened: The store was bought by Long & McQuade. We were all devastated and in fear for our jobs. But in fact it turned out to be the greatest thing that happened. I learned quickly from my new boss that the way I was treated was unacceptable which was very eye opening to me I had trained myself to be the whipping post for so long that I just excepted the behaviour as normal. My new boss would point out the bad behaviour and say to me "This is not right at all no one deserves to be treated like this especially you" He would also say "Darcy we will change the way things are here over time". My new boss taught me so much about patience and how to motivate people in the work place and bring about change slowly. But firmly.

Over the first couple of weeks I went from just doing Guitar repairs and sales to shipping and receiving, credit checking rentals and financial agreements, ordering stock and staging all the store displays for big sales promotions, scheduling hours, health and safety, bank deposits basically running the store. I got health benefits, a pension plan and a trip to the Taylor Guitar factory in San Diego. I was learning quickly that the way I was treated in the past was not expectable. I deserved to be treated better then I was. The stress of all my new jobs plus the sever state of depression I was in and the reality that I had been treated badly by my so called friends for so long in the work place lead to my total break down at work. Crying everyday in my office, feeling over whelmed by my work load, wanting to disappear every day, walking out of the store only to turn around and come back in and continue to work in the this sever state of depression. It was too much for me to handle. After 3 months of working in this environment I was a mess and that's when the big day happened and I made the call to get help. My good friend and co- worker whom I had talked to and who had been watching me slowly break down over this time forced me to make the call to get help.

After my new boss observed this environment at work and told me so many times how the behaviour of my old boss and my friends in the store was unacceptable and I started to notice it as well. Things that I had just let get said and disliked I stood up for myself. When my old boss would say "I liked the fat Darcy better he was more fun to be around when he laughed his fat would giggle and he would sweat all the time even if he was just walking around" I would say "I like the new me much better."

The problem was that I kept this thing going for too long I wasn't the brunt of all the jokes and I wasn't a whipping post for laughter I was a human being and I was a good father and husband and a good employee who handled some much of the work load in the store that it consumed me. I took it home with me and I was finished with it.

By this time, it was a year after we got bought out and a year since I had started therapy. My new boss gave me responsibilities and I followed thru with them and believe it or not he made me the assistant manager of the store. The person who was the brunt of all the jokes, whom everyone treated as a fool for so long, was now in charge of things. I wasn't a fool after all.

I now had tools to change who I was and I was ready to use them.

I remember I was talking with a good friend of mine, a sales rep, in my repair shop and he told me something that has stuck in my mind ever since. "Darcy," he said, "Where you work is not who you are!" I was blown away because for so long I had always taken work home with me. I let these co-workers take so much of me for so long. But the humiliation and the jokes were wrong, and the person they were making fun of, I wasn't that person at all.

Where I work is not who I am, and I was about to prove that to myself with some strong actions. This is how I did it.

The past is the past.

I no longer work at that place where I was humiliated for so long. I am not the person I was then. I had to stop being that person and start being my true self, no matter how hard it seemed. I started with the things that bothered me and I created thought records and journal entries on them and I proved those people wrong.

If a comment was made about my old weight and how I was different when I was fat, I would stand up for myself and say, "I like who I am, and that's what matters."

Then I would do a journal entry after and it would go like this.

I stood up for myself when a comment was made about my old weight and how that person liked me more when I was fat. I feel proud that I have lost this weight. I fought hard to lose it and no one can take that away from me. If this person thinks so little of me now, who cares? That person is not my friend. I only work with him. What he says doesn't mean thing.

I would prove these thoughts and actions wrong all day. If someone said "Remember when Darcy ate 12 slices of pizza for 20 bucks and we all laughed and it was so much fun. Darcy was so much fun back then." I would say to them, "I am glad that humiliating myself brought you so much joy."

Then I would write in my journal:

The past is the past. I am not the clown anymore and I will never be one again. I no longer look for happiness at my own expense. I will never let these people do this to me again. I am not a clown. Where I work is not who I am.

The Journal entries work so well and are so inspiring and uplifting.

Thought record:

Work

Sit:

Where I work and what I do for a paycheck is not who I am.

Mood:

Happy 100% Confident 100%

Thoughts:

I am a hard worker.

I am a strong man.

l am a leader in my workplace.

I am good father and a good husband.

I can't control the outcome of things at work. All I can do is to keep on working and doing my job and not stress when things don't go the way I want them to. It will only make me sick and I will spiral down, and I am happier not being depressed!

This is a Journal entry from Christmas dinner with store staff.

I need to talk about who I am.

At my work party, all my friends were telling my new boss about all the funny things I did years ago, and about how much fun and how happy and jolly I used to be when I was fat. And now I'm no fun anymore.

It really bothers me that they only liked me back then because I made a fool of myself and I clowned around to make them laugh. I did humiliating things so they would laugh and like me. I hated it.

The more I work on myself the more I realize that I didn't like being that man. Now it's funny, because my old boss misses me being the clown and the brunt of all his jokes. He says things like, "Back in the good old days when Darcy was fat and jolly and fun to be around…" He doesn't respect me at all and he is disappointed that I'm not there to make fun of anymore.

Things I did at work.

When I was fat, I would run on the spot for my coworkers, and sing a stupid song while I did it, so they would laugh at me. When I was out of shape, I would sweat while working, just moving boxes around, and co-workers would laugh at how out of shape I was. When people brought in donuts, I would eat more than I should because it would make them laugh.

All these things were done in the past and there is no one to blame but myself. The thing here is that I am drawing a line in the sand. The change may take time, but little by little I will be myself. That clown will be gone forever.

The key to stopping this whole thing has always been in my hands. I had to tell people that I disliked this talk and that that clown wasn't who I really was. In life, we have to make it known how we wish to be treated and if people still treat you in a way you dislike, then action must be taken. To take a stand in life, and to ask for help in taking a stand, takes courage and strength. I still struggle with what is said at work but it is in my power to change. I am getting stronger and I have faith that I will be myself one day. If being myself means losing these so-called friends, then that is on them, because I have no choice but to be myself. That is my lifelong dream and I am not stopping.

The next step was to actually take breaks at work, which was something I had not done in the full year I was working for Long & McQuade. To work up to that, before work I would get a coffee and just relax before starting. I would think of nothing and smile and enjoy my alone time. Then at lunch I would do the same. At noon I would walk out the front door and go to the coffee shop to eat my lunch and just relax for 30 minutes and think about nothing at all.

It took a lot of work to do that. I had been living for work for so long that even at lunch I would be thinking about what repairs I had to do and if any shipments need to go out and if any orders for customers had come in. It was hard to turn off, but I would use my safe place sometimes. I would go to the tree, step inside and disappear. I was gone. All the work worries could wait till I got back there. It was only guitars and amps and things like that. I am a human being I am more important than some one's *Stratocaster* or *Les Paul* guitar.

Next my good friend Nelson used to drive me home from work and on the drive home we would talk about work and all the things that pissed us off. Then I would get out of the car and because of that conversation with in the car, I would still be stuck at work. I was bringing work home with me. So I started to walk home instead, to clear my head. I would take deep breaths and even use this time to go to my safe place and just relax and be a tree. And when I got home, work was gone.

Everything from that place was not worth thinking about. I have a wife and a son whom I love and when I am home I want to be with them. So, bang! Work is gone when I get home. There are no thoughts of guitars and amps and sales and numbers and rentals and blah! blah! blah! I also began to spend less time with my friends from work. I didn't want to do that, because they are my friends, but I found that hanging out with them lead to work talk. When I was home, I wanted to be finished with work. So my friends would have to wait till I was ready to hang with them. I wasn't ready yet, but I would be sooner or later, after learning to separate my work life and my home life.

I started doing something on a whim one day. We have to wear uniforms to work and I really don't like that, but it's part of the job, so I do. We wear black pants and a Long & McQuade shirt or a shirt and tie. So I started to wonder, how can I do more to leave work at work? I tried a simple thing before work starts I wear one of my own t shirts, a shirt I would normally wear when I am not working. The problem with uniforms is you become your work and yourself image is lost, which is a huge thing. Leaving my house already belonging to Long & McQuade is wrong. When walking to work I am Darcy Patrick, not the assistant manager yet, and not the sales guy or guitar guy. I am me. So I wear the t shirt to work and when the store opens at 10:00 I go into my office and I put on my work shirt and I start work. When I go for lunch I change my shirt and go for lunch. I get back and on goes the Long &McQuade shirt. After work I change back into my t shirt and I am free from work and I don't take work home anymore.

Where I work is not who I am. Even talking about work when I am at home had to stop. We all have issues about where we work. That is just the way it is: we spend most our day at work. It is good to talk to your wife or friends if you are having a hard time at work, but know when to stop. Live in the now. You'll find that work will just fade away and that what is important is what happens after work, enjoying your free time. Enjoy just forgetting work till Monday. Work will be there when you get back. Forgetting about it is actually fun. What isn`t fun is wasting free time by taking work home with you.

Take pride in your free time. Enjoy life and have fun. Work is just work. It is not your life; it is just what helps you pay bills and live the way you want to. The key is living life, not working all the time, because you have only this life to live. Being stuck in work sucks. Leave work at work!!

Sometimes I just write in my journal "where I work is not who I am" sometimes I will write it 10 times in a day just to remind me because it seems we all forget this all the time!! Where you work is not who you are!!

Running head on into the past!!! (EMDR)

Journal entry:

I was ready to talk.

These are my so-called tragedies:

Having my hand injured in a car accident that my best friend and I should have never walked away from and having it impact my whole life with two surgeries and pain all the time every day.

Not being able to talk. Stuttering and not pronouncing my R's.

Switching high school and thinking I could just be a different person and just having the same shit happen over and over again.

Barely graduated from high school and barely made it into college. I really struggle with tests and performance anxiety, even though I play every weekend in a band.

I fail at a lot of things.

I failed grade 3... I let it change who I was and how I thought about myself. I stopped talking to friends and let myself separate from them. I took life too seriously, in fear of failing over and over again

I hold very high values and when I do not succeed to my unrealistic goals, I feel it is the end of the world.

I tried to become a cop, a lifelong dream. I wrote tests and failed them. I tried to get into the RCMP and failed....

I found out that I was sterile, with not one drop of sperm in me a count of zero after coming from a family that had lots of children. There are hundreds in my blood line, and I have a mutated gene of CF which dates so far back there is no sign of it in my blood line.

We spent lots of money trying to get pregnant and I even took the blame for that not going right. How I don't know but I did.

I have failed over and over again.

I hardly ever see any fruits to my labor in anything I do. People ride my back and I do all the hard work because they know I am more than capable of doing mindless tasks and I do them fast and well. So while people are gaining things and getting praise, I am working and working, in the background, never being seen.

I want to change that.

I view my life as an ongoing tragedy. I concentrate on the negative and romancing bad things till they are larger than life I worry about shit that normal people don't even think about.

I want to be happy, to be who I am, to be myself, for the first time in my life.

In college I sat on the side lines and allowed my friends to take advantage of me all the time.

I worked in a music store and I was the butt of every joke, every day. I smiled and acted like a clown and slowly just withdrew into myself and acted like nothing was wrong... when I was drowning the whole time.

Life has its ups and downs and round and rounds....

Take my son, for instance. We saved him and brought him into our house. He is the light of my life and I am so thankful for him. He is everything to me. But still I sometimes feel like a failure, and even though I am not, I let it bring me down.

But now at least I am talking about it and I am seeing things for what they are and not for what I make them out to be.

There was a list of things I wanted to talk about and heal from my past. I was ready to take these things on now with my new tools and my ability to prove myself wrong. It was go time. My therapist told me she thought that I was the perfect candidate for EMDR therapy. What is EMDR therapy? Here is a short description. (**By Kristen Stewart | Medically reviewed by Pat F. Bass III, MD, MPH, everydayhealth.com**)

> "The EMDR approach involves eight phases that generally start with the therapist taking a thorough client history, establishing a rapport with the patient, and explaining the procedure over the span of a few sessions before actual treatment begins. During the treatment itself, the patient focuses on the traumatic event and accompanying sensations while also following the therapist's fingers with his or her eyes as the fingers are moved back and forth. (The fingers are most often used, but some therapists use auditory tones or tapping instead.) This is then repeated numerous times until the patient does not feel distress when thinking about the upsetting memory."

I was scared going into EMDR. It was a lot of work preparing for it. We talked about a lot of things that I had been unable to talk about before. But I did talk about them and we made a game plan to start.

We did a full history of when I began not being myself, and all the things that had happened after that, leading me to where I am now. It was pretty in depth. I was very, very, very scared of going back to these places and looking them in the eye. But that is what it would take to heal the damage done by these life changing events. I had a safe place to go to when it got to frightening and I also had all these new ways of taking charge of events and dealing with them.

After so many years of running away, I was running toward these things and I was scared but ready!!

I was going to succeed and win and that's who I am now a winner.....

EMDR

Where to start? This part of this book is the hardest for me to talk about and the most personal.

When I was young I could not pronounce the letter R and that makes even saying your name out loud a stressful event when your name is Darcy and it comes out as "Docy". I was 6 in Grade 1. I was so self-conscious about how I talked that it was crushing. Just talking at times made my classmates break out laughing and I was crushed and it killed my self-esteem before I even knew who I was in life.

I also started stuttering and tripping over my words because of the anxiety I had before even opening my mouth to read out loud or answer a question. I was looked at as stupid, or so I thought and speech therapy did not help. I was taken out of class for speech therapy three times a week. It was a joke. The young lady teaching me how to talk would work with me for 10 minutes and then let me draw pictures of trucks for the rest of the time. She did nothing for me. She would get frustrated with my progress and give up.

So we went back to that classroom where it all started.

My therapist put head phones on me and I heard beeps that went from one ear to the next. We used the five senses to retrieve what I remembered from that time (just like the safe place). My therapist asked me, when I think of this place, what do I feel? I told her, I feel humiliated and weak.

I breathed deeply and relaxed. She asked me what I saw. I told her I was in a class room filled with little kids, my friends and we were introducing ourselves to a priest. It was my turn to tell him my name and I said Docy and the class laughed. I said it again and the class laughed. The priest made me say it again and this time the girl behind me told him my name was Darcy and said I couldn't talk, which was not true.

The emotion was over whelming and I was crying like I have never cried before. Then I was in a room with that damn speech therapist and she was trying to teach me to say the letter R... And then I remembered sitting in my bedroom and watching myself talk and working on my speech by myself looking in a mirror. In my memory, I bounced all over the place and I cried a lot, which was very, very good. All this emotion from years gone past just flowed out of me, emotion that had been locked away, trapped inside me since grade school.

I was emptying the barrel.....

I went back to a time in school when we had to do an assignment about what we wanted to be when we grew up. I was sitting and looking down at my red binder and reading my title page. I could see the pink eraser and my blue pen. I had to stand up in class and give this speech. I got up and was shaking and I told the class what I wanted to be more than anything was myself and I remember the teacher stopped me and asked me if that was what I was going to talk about and I said yes and she told me to sit down and gave me a failing mark that day. That's the moment, I told my therapist. That is the moment in life where I stopped 100% being myself.

I was crying and crying. I was actually feeling for the first time.

Moment after humiliating moment I watched and cried and I and went to my safe place to calm down and it worked. Then I would go back again and remember more and more about grade school and about how I went to a different high school than my friends to start over again but it didn't change a thing. It was always the same and now after all these tears and all these bad memories flooding me I decided to jump in and help that poor little boy I was back then.

It seemed strange but I walked into that class room and took myself by the hand. I walked out of that school and over to the bike racks where my bike was parked. I got on my knees and I talked to that little boy.

I told him that everyone was wrong, that he wasn't stupid, and that he was smart. I told him that he could talk and that he was going to grow up to be a good father, a good husband, and a great bass player. He was going to grow up and go to college to study music and be a professional musician and teach children out of his house. He was going to buy a house from playing music. He would chase a dream of being a police officer, even test for it. I told him that being yourself is a lifelong goal and now at 42 I was learning to be myself and that I am succeeding!!!

Everyone was wrong. It's was okay for him (me) to just leave this bad place! After 36 years I was finally ready to leave this place and just move on with my life. I wasn't stupid I wasn't a waste of time...

So as we stood by the bike racks, I pictured myself getting on my bike and riding it to the end of the street, just around the corner from my house when I was growing up. I sat on the rocks overlooking Lake Ontario as I had done so many times before, during my childhood. I cried my ass off and I emptied that barrel of emotion. I saved that little boy. I pulled him out of that place and now I am free. I'm not that child anymore and now it is time for me to heal.

I have a lot to work on but I am emptying that barrel...

Then I was running along the beach we always go to on vacation and I could see the golden sand as I ran along the shore line, like I do every day on vacation. I felt free and I reported what I did to my therapist. She asked me if I wanted to go to my safe place again and I went to that tree. She asked me, when I think about where we went, how did I feel? I told her I felt strong and free. She asked me where I felt that. I told her I felt it deep in my heart!

I stepped out of the tree I open my eyes and I was free....

So that was my first EMDR and I felt exhausted. It took me quite a few days to recover. I would write down journal entries if I had any triggers from the experience but there were no triggers. I was amazed at the work I had done and the fact that, after all this time, I had finally left that place of pain. The pain was gone. I don't know why I had held on to this memory and let it sculpt my whole life, but I did and now it was gone. I was never stupid and I was never a failure and I *am* able to talk. I should be proud of myself because I actually fixed my own speech, working on it in the mirror by myself in my bedroom.

The greatest thing I got from this 1ˢᵗ EMDR experience was actually letting go. The one thing I was afraid of all along was letting my emotions go, but now I am sitting right here in my office writing about it!!

I didn't go crazy I didn't have a nervous breakdown.

I am fine.

I can feel emotion I now!! I know how to deal with it. I have tools and I am strong and I am ready to be myself, my lifelong dream.

This is a journal which I emailed my therapist before we went on to the next EMDR session:

> If I'm going to do EMDR on the car accident I was in, before we do it I need to tell you more about what happened and how it changed my life and how I saved my best friend's life, my friend since I was 4 years old.
>
> I need to address this. But I can't do it like before. I have to be able to talk to you as it is happening because the whole experience is so vivid and terrifying that I am scared to do it...
>
> *Everything is frozen in time. I can still taste the dirt in my mouth. I can hear the song that was playing in the car be for it rolled. I can smell the swamp where the car landed. I still see everything in motion from the time the car went out of control, the end-over-end rolling. The moment is still there in my mind.*
>
> I need to heal this. But I need to be able to talk while I do that.
>
> I haven't blocked this out. I think of it all the time. I lost so much because of that day. I am scared to go there and see it all again... I saved Mark's life. He has two beautiful girls and a beautiful wife. We were just kids then, still in high school, in Grade 11. I was 18. 24 years have gone by and it still terrifies me. Sometimes it will run through my head and I start to sweat and my hands shake. I feel trapped and my heart races...

The accident seemed to last a long time. While it was happening, everything slowed down. That's how I was able to grab Mark's head and pull him down on to me. The top of the car was crushed flat and my left hand was crushed instead of Marks head rupturing the tendon on my ring finger and breaking the knuckle, I was trapped for a short time before I was able to get out.

I know you can help me with this and I want to heal this, but I can't feel alone while I do it. I need to know I can talk to you while I do it.

My left hand is a mess. I had two operations on it and I play in pain every time I play. I auditioned for college in pain and played through college in pain. My left hand is half the size of my right hand. Lately, it is seizing up from the two operations. The pain is constant. Every time I play my bass I remember the accident so vividly. We should have been killed that day. The car was destroyed. The police couldn't believe we survived.

We walked through another swamp to get to a house on the hill. My face was cut up bad and I couldn't move or feel my hand the pain was so bad.

This was a terrifying event. It was bloody and traumatic, both physically and mentally. It is just something I am not willing to bring back up in this book in detail, like I did the school EMDR. I have closed this and healed it. But I will share the beautiful way in which I turned the memory around, to demonstrate how powerful my new way of thinking is and how using thought records can be the best way to fight off depression.

Here is the record.

Thought record:

My hand

I got hurt in that car accident. My hand is damaged for life.

So many things happened because of that day, good and bad. But now the bad things are gone. The many good things that happened are here still and now I see them.

I lied about us being drunk to the police and I fixed things by sinking all the beer and whisky bottles in the swamp before the police came. I came up with the story to tell the police and we both stuck to it so Mark would not lose his driver's licence or worse. Now I realize that what I did was for a better good....

An injured hand:: I saved a life

Mark is alive. He is my best friend. He is a good husband, and a good father. He has two beautiful little girls. I was saved as well that day, and I have a wonderful wife and son whom I love. I am so happy with my son. He is the light of my life. Our children grow up together, just like Mark and I did. They will have so many good memories together, just like Mark and I do.

When I now deal with the accident, I look to all the good that has come from my hand being damaged forever and realize all these good things that have come from this incredible story, this accident that no one should have walked away from.

The feeling that I am responsible for all that is happening now brings a smile to my face. Instead of feeling robbed, I feel empowered and strong.

I grabbed Mark's head and pull him down as the car rolled end over end. My hand was crushed his head was not. We walked away...

I think I have a clearer outlook on what happened that day. I know the value of what was lost and what was saved.

A hurt hand verses us both dead and no future for my son. No Erin or Emma, Mark's daughters. Well, I can live with my hand being hurt and I can now move on and leave this behind me.

I am at peace with that horrible day, with the blood and the years of pain, with the lying to the police and the sinking of the beer and whisky bottles making up the story and fixing thing's so mark didn't get charged or lose his driver's licence. It's all over now.

I'm free from it.

When I read this record it means so much to me, because in this record I took the most gruesome day and the most terrifying thing that could have happened and I turned it around. After years of reliving it and feeling sorry for myself because of my hand being so hurt, I now just look at it as a good thing. It is no longer a terrible thing that has destroyed my life, but an experience that has actually made my life.

Now when my hand hurts when I play my bass, I am reminded of life. New life. My son and my wife, and Mark's daughters and his wife. I am reminded of how we walked away from that twisted pile of steel. I don't feel robbed at all. I feel like a hero!!

Dealing with failure was one of my last EMDR's.

When I was a little boy, and even as I grew up, I always wanted to be a police officer. Not just any police officer – I wanted to be in the RCMP, Canada's finest. But I was so convinced that I was stupid and unable to read and write, being a police officer was nothing but a silly dream. So I let it die away and just stay a dream.

When I was 35, I started to run and work out. I lost a lot of weight and I was feeling very confident and so I took a chance and started testing for the police and for the RCMP. I studied my ass off, reading books and took online police and RCMP courses. I did great at the physical part of it. Hell, I was out running 24 year old men and women with ease. It was funny.

At test time, I was in trouble. I was hardly able to fill out the personal information part of the test without screwing that up. Then the tests would start and I would just look at the paper and think about grade school and how this was just a big waste of time and how I was the same stupid boy I was back then. I tested for the police once and failed. But the RCMP was what I was after. I tested twice for that and failed each time. It was crushing to say the least. My track record was adding up to failure after failure I was a joke a waste of time and flesh.

So it was EMDR time and I was ready to heal one more thing.

My therapist took me back to the testing room.

There was this 20 foot long oval shape table and there were 20 of us sitting around it, waiting for our test. There I was, sitting with these 25- and 26-year olds. Young men and women, college educated and smart as can be. I looked down and saw the info sheet in front of me I was shaking like a leaf overcome by nerves and feeling like an outsider in this room. I had no clue what I was going to do to even deal with this over whelming fear of this place. How I would heal these events.

I remembered filling out the information sheet in pencil and the young woman beside me telling me I was supposed to use the pen, not the pencil. The pencil was for the test. I panicked and erased all I had written and did it again in pen. My page was a mess. It looked just horrible and my hand writing was just as bad. I was a failure before I started.

Then the instructor came in and opened the windows and it was freezing. The place was cold and the breeze was blowing right on my back.

I was reliving the whole RCMP testing again, just image after image and question after question and panic attack after panic attack while we did this EMDR. I was flashing back to grade school and high school and not being able to read and not being able to talk just thoughts of failure and being a loser.

Then even while I was remembering all of this, I had had enough and I took a stand! Something started to happen to me in my therapist's office. I started to use the tools I have now. I went back to that RCMP test and I proved myself wrong. I countered the thoughts I was having while I wrote these tests.

> The info sheet I filled out in pencil.

> *There were no instructions for me to use the pen and I only made a mess of the page because I erased it all and had to rush through it and do it all over again in pen in half the time, before the instructor came in. I panicked and let my nerves get the best of me.*

> I was sitting at a table with these young people right out of college. I had no right to be there. I was stupid and old.

I had every right to be there. I took online tests and courses and passed the tests with 90's. I had studied for 12 months while working full time and gigging 3 nights a week. I deserved to be there.

Question after question, I second guessed every answer while writing that test. I just thought about failing tests back in grade school and never really gave myself a fair chance at all.

I had no chance at passing these tests. I was in no state to write at all. I was an emotional mess and unable to think properly at all.

Looking back at that test was such an eye opener. I am not that man at all now. I was beaten down by depression and had zero self-esteem. I was put in a high stress situation with no tools to help me at all but I expected to pass those high pressure tests for the RCMP. Come on. I proved myself wrong again. I was not a failure at all. I had had no chance. That made me look at who I had become, at how much I have accomplished just in the last year.

I am a failure.

No I am not I made the call for help and I work hard every day and use my tools to fight off depression. After one year of working for Long and McQuade, I am an assistant manager and I am going to level 4 management training. Long and Mcquade only sends 16 people a year out of 64 stores a year. I am far from a failure.

In EMDR, I kept proving myself wrong over and over again. In my head I countered all my negative thoughts from that time when I was writing the police tests. When I finally finished proving myself wrong over and over again I went to my safe place and just thought of nothing but taking in air through my leaves and out through my roots. I stayed in the tree till I felt I was ready, and then I did the last thing I needed to do.

I have a house we go to sometimes to help close out the therapy sessions. It's a meditation exercise. A glass house sits in the middle of a beautiful, green grass field surrounded by a forest of tall trees.

This house is a peaceful place. It is a laboratory where some large bottles with water in them are kept. They are all labeled with words that represent my emotions, good and bad. I take the bad emotion that I am dealing with and I empty out that bottle and I wash it up and I fill it with clean water. I put a new label on it and take a nice long drink from it, letting this new emotion fill me up. Then I place this new bottle on a clean shelf with other bottles I have done the same with. I like to sit in an office chair and look out at the forest till I am at peace. Then I open my eyes and I am free.

This time I had something special for the bottle, called failure. That bottle has been hidden for so long. I took it and emptied its black, dirty water down the drain, but then I did something different with it. This time I placed that bottle in the garbage. I had no use for it anymore. it was time to just say "Good bye". I didn't even want to reuse it as a container for the new emotion. I asked Mastora if I could just get a new bottle and label it success and she said, "Of course you can." So I walked over to the closet and opened the door and there were hundreds of new, clean bottles for me to fill!! I took one and put the label on and wrote "Success" on it. I filled it up and drank from it and I cried and I know I am not a failure. Never was, never will be.

I walked over to the office chair and I smiled with joy. I sat there peacefully. Mastora asked how much I still believed I was a failure after this EMDR. I told her, "Zero." She asked me, when I think of these Police and RCMP tests now what do I feel. I told her I feel strong and I feel smart and I feel these feelings in my heart to be 100% true. I opened my eyes and I am free from failure.

Back when I was writing those tests, I was lost and beaten down by depression and I really had no chance to pass. But I am at peace with it now. I chased a dream I had had since child hood and I take pride in the fact that I tried. Not many people get a chance to chase their dreams. I hope one or two of those young men and women passed and made it into the RCMP and made their dreams come true!

EMDR future template.

Today at therapy we talked about things that might happen to me in the future and how I was going to deal with situations that will happen. It was reinforced to me that I will always have to do thought records and I will always have to keep my tools ready to use. My life is a constant fight to stay up and to stay positive. I have had 38 years of negative thinking and only 1 year of therapy and changing my thought patterns. Although I am doing very well I have a long way to go.

Working on using my tools is like practising music. It means learning when to use each tool and not panicking and not getting over whelmed. For each situation I am in there is a tool or tools I can use. There is no right or wrong just what works for me.

Mastora and I talked about situations that will happen. We talked in great detail, just as if I was there, experiencing it in real time.

She asked me what tools I would use. I answered and she gave input as well we brain-stormed together. We came up with different ways of dealing with different situations. She gave me home work to come up with a bunch of situations that will happen to me and my task was to bring those to her at our next session.

Here is one situation:

Going to the CF clinic in Toronto:

When I go to the CF clinic in Toronto, from the beginning to the end of the trip I am faced with so many things that would spiral me into a bad place, beginning with the drive. The highway is stressful enough, never mind being in the heart of Toronto. I am triggered before I even get to the hospital. So I learn to use the following tools to deal with the drive itself.

> I leave really early, about 1 hour earlier than I normally would, just to put my mind at ease. I get a coffee and put one of my favorite CDs on in the car to relax me. I treat myself well while I drive. While driving to the clinic I practise my breathing exercises to stay as calm as I can. I just relax and drive, not thinking about anything else. I look at the scenery and control my breathing, not thinking of anything but the drive there.

> When I get there I am seated in a hall way and there are doctors everywhere going from room to room and talking among themselves. It is a high-paced and high-stress place. It

makes me feel overwhelmed and insufficient. When I finally
get into a room to see a doctor there are four of them and
they all have different jobs and they all have lots of questions
for me and tests to run.

I need to relax and breathe deep while I am in the hallway.
I need to shut the world out, go to my safe place and just
be my tree and not let any of the world in at all. I block out
the running around and the stress and the hustle and bustle.
Once I am in the room and the questions start from all the
different doctors, I need to realize that they are here to help
and I need to see how lucky I am to have so many smart
and specialized doctors here in one room just for me. They
are here to help and if they learn from me being here and
the research they are doing can help other people that is a
good thing.

I always have to go for blood tests, which are on the other
side of the hospital. I am put in a huge waiting room with 100
people all waiting for blood work to be done. But I have a
schedule to keep. I have other tests on other floors to be done
and if I don't get back in time for them then the whole day
is shot.

Again here I need to stop the spiral. I have tools to stop the panic which
always sets in. I have to get out my phone do a thought record and just slow
things down.

Thought record:

Blood tests

If I don't get these blood tests done in time the rest of the day is shot. I can't be
late. I drove all this way and took a day off work. I can't miss any more work. If I
don't get in soon then I am fucked.

*I will be on time. I gave them my schedule when I gave them my paper work and they
know I have to be at other tests at other times. This happens all the time here. I have*

to calm down and just relax and even go to my tree and breathe deeply and wait for my name to be called. Think about nice things and relax everything will be fine.

Once my name is called, I have to get what seems like 50 vials of blood taken and drink this orange drink. I dislike needles, but the drink is super sweet, which isn't bad at all. I love sweet things.

While they take my blood, I keep calm by talking to the nurse who is doing the job. I ask her how her day is going and how long she is working till. I keep my mind busy by talking to her. It works. I distract myself with the conversation and I am sure she doesn't mind. I bet people do this all the time. In no time at all the blood is taken and I am off.

Next I have to get a bunch of x-rays of my lungs and that is a long wait in a different part of the hospital again.

I pass my time by writing in my journal about how the day is going and what tools I am using to stay up and not spiral, so I can read later on and see how good a job I did on this stress-filled day. The day is stress-filled but I am going to conquer the stress.

Next I go into what I call the "breathing bubble", where I do all these breathing exercises with a head set on. There are many wires attached to me. It is stressful and enclosed and uncomfortable.

Here I just do what the person tells me to do. I listen to her voice and I do the breathing. I think of it as breathing exercises and I just relax and go with the flow. There is no passing or failing these tests. I have nothing to prove. I am here so they can get information to help me and see if I have lost any lung capacity since I was there last.

When the breathing bubble is over, it's another round of blood work and back to see the doctors. This is where it always goes downhill. They talk to me about my tests and how my lung capacity has shrunk and that my blood sugar is bad and my blood pressure is high. They all take turns having at me then they write me prescriptions and send me on my way. I feel like a Guinea Pig. I feel down and depressed. My health is failing and I am a loser and I am going to die from this sooner or later and why did I even come here in the first place?

I stop and use all my tools before I spiral big time. I walk a block down the street to the city park that I have gone to before and I close my eyes and I take deep breaths and I go to my tree. I take the air in through my leaves and out through my roots. I let the wind blow through me and move me side to side I get lost in the moment and let the world fade away, just like I always do when I am in my safe place. I sit there for as long as I want to. My day is done. I am in no hurry to leave and get stuck in traffic. I just sit there and let all the stress leave me and fade away. When I am ready I step out and I open my eyes and I am relaxed and centered.

Now I get my phone out and I write about my day once again. I write down how nice it is to have so many doctors concerned about my health and how lucky I am that I have this place to go to, to keep track off my health and my CF. I also write how nice these people are and how they answered all my questions. If I ever do get sick, they will be there to help me. I also think about the research they are doing on CF and how maybe they will learn something from me and save some people's lives that have full blown CF.

I also take the time to read my early journal entries I wrote that day to see just how strong I am and how I used my tools all day to stop myself from spiraling. I feel proud now, because this day is usually a total write-off. It usually means a big spiral downwards. I am feeling so good about myself and how I battled through this, I am actually smiling.

And that was my homework: to come up with a future situation and imagine using my tools to beat the spiral. I think I did a really good job and I think that when I have to go to the clinic I will be fine if I use my tools like I did here.

The future template is actually fun because you can test yourself and come up with great ways to use your tools. Realizing that I will have to use my tools for the rest of my life isn't a bad thing at all. I can fight now and before I never could. I know I can win with practice and more practice.

EMDR is a great tool, too. It has helped me a lot. There were many other EMDR sessions and I worked through a lot of things. I am stronger and have a better outlook on life and I have healed past trauma. Now I am able to move forward. I can avoid having the past bring me down. I am no longer running from anything. I am Kicking at the darkness!! And it`s bleeding daylight

My affirmations

When my therapist told me to make affirmations for myself, it was kind of funny because of this *Saturday Night Live* skit that I used to watch. The skit featured a guy sitting in a chair. His name was Stuart Smallie and he would look into mirror and say silly things about himself and people would laugh. The skit was very popular at the time. So I was kind of taken back by what we were doing in this session.

It kind of felt like a joke to me and I really didn't want to feel humiliated or embarrassed at therapy or look like a fool like Stuart Smallie did when he said his silly things. But I was open to anything that could help me and so far everything has worked even though I didn't think it would.

I was told to come up with five affirmations that I believed in, and write them down. These affirmations seemed silly at first, but they are actually my lifelong goals now. They help me all the time and I write them down in my journal every day. Sometimes I even say them out loud to remind me who I am. They help me get through tough days. Here are my affirmations. They are unique to me and I will explain each one and why I have it.

- **I succeed in life.**

This has been a major thorn in my side. In the past, I only looked at my failures and never my triumphs. Saying this affirmation made me think about the things

I have succeeded at. The wording is so important here. There is no doubt in the phrase and to say it makes me feel good.

I succeed in life. Writing it and believing it and saying it out loud is so empowering .Thinking of just the things I have succeed at, it blows me away at times how I overlooked all the good and let the bad bring me down for so long. What a power full thing writing and speaking something can be. When we were young we were taught a phrase that was so wrong: "Sticks and stones will break my bones, but names will never hurt me." What a lie!! But it works both ways. Words can hurt, but they can help enormously, too. Saying things over and over and writing them over and over and believing those words works!

I succeed in life. So simple, but so powerful.

- **I am worth changing.**

It breaks my heart when I say this one and write it, because for so long I felt that I wasn't worth changing. It has been such an uphill battle, learning and fighting, but this phrase is right! I am worth changing.

I am learning to love myself. I am learning to value myself. I am worth changing. I am worth the time and money. To invest in one's own self is the greatest investment of all. Change is a good thing and knowing that you are worth changing is the first step.

Many times I felt I was not worth the skin I was in, but not anymore. Now I know different. I am worth changing and everyone is worth changing. Everyone deserves to be forgiven. I've got news for you: the most important thing is you need to forgive yourself. Realizing that you're worth changing is the first and foremost thing. I am worth changing!!

- **I deserve to be happy. I am not afraid to be happy!**

"I deserve to be happy". What is that? For so long happiness was so far out of reach. Even emotion was at times out of reach. But I've got good news: everyone deserves to be happy. Whether it is playing with your son or sitting quietly on your back porch with your wife, not talking at all, just holding hands and loving each other. Happiness is something we all deserve in life. Some people need to learn that it is okay to feel happy. That's okay. What comes naturally to some doesn't to others and that's where the "I am not afraid to be happy" affirmation comes in.

I was so afraid to show emotion at all, never mind happiness, that anything was out of reach. I could act like I was happy. Hell, I was the best actor of all time. But not anymore. I am setting myself free and this phrase proves it to me. How strong is it?? Just say it with me and you'll see

I DESERVE TO BE HAPPY! I AM NOT AFRAID TO BE HAPPY!

It works. I know it does. I say it every day!

- **I am not afraid to be myself.**

This one is scary.

I had lived for so long just trying to make other people happy. Everything I was about was making people happy. All I ever did was to make friends and make people like me. It was time for me to be myself and I was ready because this phrase says I am.

"I am not afraid to be myself"

I am not afraid is the key. Now I stick to it. I will say this in my head whenever I feel that I need to or when I am in a situation where I would normally bend and break, rather than be myself. I just say it and set myself free.

"I am not afraid to be myself" and if people don't like who I am then it doesn't matter because not everyone is going to like me and now I can live with that. I can live with the fact that some of my friends may not like me and may not be my friends after all. I can live with the fact that I love who I am, and seeking approval for things I do is wrong and always has been. And guess what? "I deserve to be happy." "I am not afraid to be happy." "I am not afraid to be myself."

- **I am a strong and smart man and I will beat depression.**

The best was saved for last. All through school, both grade school and high school, and then college, I was convinced I was stupid and less of a person than I really was.

My whole life I was searching for approval from others and never having any faith in myself. I had no self-esteem. But that is not true anymore

"I am a strong and smart man." I believe that. I have worked hard at everything I have ever tried. Sometimes I failed and sometimes I succeeded. That has made me both strong and smart, because now I know so much about myself from all the hard work and from never giving up.

I have chased so many of my dreams and I fell short, but in doing so I learned so much. I stood at the edge and I looked down and I turned my back and ran. I left that bridge that same day I held my son in my arms for the first time. I was strong enough to pick up a phone one day and call for help. I stopped beating myself up day after day, and I have worked hard as I always do at everything I try.

These are my affirmations! I say them every day I also end all my thought records and journal enters with them repetition is always the key when using tools. When I end my thought records and journal enters with my affirmations it fills me with confidence and pride that what I wrote is something that matters and enforces the good work I have done . You can do the same: pick five for yourself and make them your own. Make them mean something, as I did so they're not empty and meaningless. Let them build you up and let yourself feel proud when you say them. Let this exercise empower you.

Some thought records and journals using Affirmations

What if's always run through my mind.

What if my pay cheque doesn't go into my bank account?

It will. It always does. It's never missed, as long as I have worked for Long and McQuade.

What if I don't get any calls for gigs?

I always do. And anyway, if the gigs don't come in then the band will end, and that might solve a problem...

What if I can't pay my bills on time?

I always pay them on time. I've never not paid a bill. They always get their money. And nothing bad will happen to me if I don't. No jail and beating, no public stoning...

What if I lose all my friends for some reason?

Don't be crazy. I have friends. I have good friends and a great family who loves me so much. And I love them. And anyway, there is no shame in losing friends. It happens and that's all there is to it. So, whatever happens, happens....

What if I lose my job?

I will find another one.

What if I get demoted?

Why would that happen? I am doing a fantastic job and everyone likes me at work. They listen to me and they come to me for help and I help them. I run the place!!

What if I have a bad day or a string of bad days? Will that mean I am back to where I started?

No. A bad day it doesn't mean a thing. I am human and I might slip, but if I do I will pull myself up and fight, using the tools I have.

What if I can't leave therapy? What if she wants me to stop going and I am not ready?

She would never stop me from seeing her. That is her job – to help me. The time between sessions is a long stretch this time, and I am having a hard time with it. But I will be fine. I will just keep living and carry on fighting and using my new tools.

What if I spiral again?

Then I will fight and use my tools!! I succeed in life! I am worth changing. I deserve to be happy. I am not afraid to be happy. I am not afraid to be myself. I am a strong and smart man. I will beat depression!!

What if's are terrible things. They run through my head so fast that I lose control of them. They overwhelm me.

I write them down and prove them wrong, the way I did here. That makes me strong and proud of myself. Proving them wrong makes the "what if's" just fade away to nothing.

The same what ifs will show up all the time and I have to prove them wrong over and over. The what if's never know when to give up.

But they'll learn because I always have the proper tools to fight them off. I will win the fight over the "what if's".

A very good day.

Today I feel good. I feel alive and well. My week has been rough, but I have worked hard and stayed cool, calm, and collected. I used the tools I have been practising with so much and they are working.

It has been a year or more since I started therapy and made the choice to fight for my life. I am proud of the choice I made. I am worth changing and I am learning to be myself and I do love who I am.

Today no matter what happens I will use my tools and I will be happy and content with the wonderful life I have made for myself. All my struggles and all my failures are lessons and I have learned from them. My life is a story of triumph and victory over everything that has come my way.

I succeed in life.

I deserve to be happy.

I am worth changing

I am a strong, smart man and I will beat depression even if it is one day at a time.

I will be myself. I am not afraid to be who I am.

Thought record:

Today I struggle...

I struggle with being involved in my life. I feel disconnected, out of touch. I am having trouble finding meaning to my life today.

Mood:

Anxiety 90%, Nervous 90%, Unsure 100%

Thoughts:

I feel I am not contributing at work. I feel like I am not doing enough, since I am a manager now.

People are coming to me for help and I am resolving problems everyday and helping my employees out and fixing guitars and amps at the same time. I am doing a good job. I am just not used to this yet. There is still a disconnection between my feelings and what is actually true at work.

I find it hard to love what I am doing and love my life today. I find it hard to concentrate on anything and I feel just blah. I feel like the grass is greener on the other side.

It is okay to feel this. At least I am feeling something. I can take joy in the fact that I can feel. Just feeling is a good thing. Just acknowledging things and feeling them is good, and even better I write them down Dealing with it is also good.

It's okay to have an off day. The good thing is I am not spiralling from it. I have come a long way and I am happy for that.

I succeed in life.

I am worth changing.

I deserve to be happy.

I will be myself. I am not afraid to be myself.

I am a strong and smart man I will beat depression.

I have come to the face the truth now. I think that I will have to fight my whole life to beat depression.

I have real good days and I have come a long way, but it seems I have to fight so much some days. It's okay. We all have bad days. It's alright to have a bad day. I have more good days than bad now and that is the greatest thing. I am proud of my fighting skills.

I succeed in life.

I deserve to be happy. I am not afraid to be happy

I am not afraid to be myself.

I am worth changing

I am a strong and smart man and I will beat depression.

Today I am overcome with emotion. I am filled with joy over the anniversary of meeting my son and I am proud of myself for working so hard and learning so much and fighting to beat depression. Happiness is filling me up and I am brought to tears in my office. For once I am crying in here and it is because of good things. I am accepting the happy feelings and it is breathtaking to say the least. "I am a strong and smart man". I believe it in my heart today! I am also proud of myself for not jumping that day and I have forgiven myself for what I was going to do. I am over joyed today!

I succeed in life.

I deserve to be happy. I am not afraid to be happy

I am worth changing

I am not afraid to be myself

I am a strong and smart man I will beat depression.

Some things are starting to happen to me, now that I am getting stronger and using my tools in living life and actually being myself. That experience is changing the way I think.

Good things are happening:

The first is I got a promotion to assistant manager of the store!

Second, and more important, my tools are working so well that my bad days and bad runs have been gone for a long time now. The most important thing of all is my new resilience. I know I will have bad times and that I will spiral some times, but I know, without a doubt in my mind, that I am strong. I will overcome whatever happens to me and I will survive.

Third and the most incredible of all, I am going to level 4 management training. My boss just called me while I was writing this! After one year working for Long and McQuade, I am going to management training! I am not a loser and I am not a failure. I succeed in life! I am learning to actually like who I am and that all this work is worth it. Spending time bettering oneself is never a waste of time and never a waste of money. I never, ever feel that I am not worth changing anymore.

I love who I am. I am proud of how far I have come since I made the call for help. I am so proud of myself right now. I am just beaming and smiling and I deserve to feel this way!

I succeed in life

I deserve to be happy, I am not afraid to be happy

I am worth changing

I am not afraid to be myself

I am a strong and smart man I will beat depression

Thought record:

Running from music

Sit:

Stop playing music it's time to step up and talk about it.

Mood:

Sad 100%, Empty 100%

When I was 11, I started playing bass guitar. I did my first gig at the age of 14 and I never stopped. I have played in countless bands. So many good musicians and so many bad ones as well. When I was young I would lie in bed at night and feel guilty if I didn't play my bass that day. I would get up and sit on my bed in the dark and practice. I was 12.

The only thing that has been a constant thing in my life is Music.

I dedicated my life to music. I made a living from it. I taught guitar and bass for 20 years. I gave guitars to underprivileged children and I taught for free as well. I have students who have children now. I fought through two hand operations to keep playing and to go to college to study music.

Now I just do it for money.

When I think back about it, I always did it for the wrong reasons. I did it to make other people happy, never myself. Now I feel the same way about music as I did the rest of my life. I need to make a change I have to stop what I am doing and help myself just like that day when I made the call for help I need to stop and remember why I even started playing because, when I play all it does for me now is trigger a spiral and I have to stop that spiralling. I am learning to acknowledge these triggers and take away their power, but playing my bass is the last trigger that I haven't dealt with. So how do I deal with this love of mine destroying me, tune after tune, gig after gig, night after night?

Maybe I need a little break. Maybe I just need to spend some time playing for myself and not for a band or a person or anything like that. Maybe I'll fall in love with music again.

Thought record:

Stopping playing music

Sit:

I used to love playing music. But now it seems to be a trigger for bad thoughts. When I play, part of me is looking for acceptance from others. When I'm on stage, all I do is think about what everyone is thinking about me and my bass playing.

Mood:

Sad 50%, Anxious 80%, Desprate60%.

Thoughts:

I could never relax and just play. When I was playing, I had a thousand thoughts running through my head. I felt like I was under a microscope, as if people were watching me, listening for me to fuck up, and when I did it was the end of the world. One bad note and I was unable to stop the downward spiral. The rest of the gig was spent watching, looking for approval from band-mates, and just thinking bad things.

Maybe it was time for me to stop playing for a while, to walk way and stop the triggering. Everyone needs a break sometimes. My health is more important than music.

But I needed the money.

I can never relax and just play. The money is a major part of my income. Without me playing there would be no vacations or money to help out. Music has me trapped. Music is supposed to set me free, not trap me.

I need to talk to someone about this but who? I had no one to talk to... So I face the music, as they say. I figured that instead, of doing thought records to prove myself wrong about the triggers I was having, I would play my bass for a while.

Facing the music

I just sat and played for fun, which was something I have never really done. I played in the mornings before a run. I never played a scale, never opened any study books. I played for the fun of it.

I used to just have goals when I played. It was always about getting something done. Learn these scales. Learn these modes, apply them to these chord changes. Learn these fake book tunes. Everyone knows these tunes off by heart, you have to know them!!

In college, music was work. It was all business all the time, never just fun playing. I always felt I was under pressure. Harmony classes, theory classes, arranging, ear training, performance classes. Three years – four with a year off trying to find someone to fix my hand so I could continue playing, continue the hard work. Now I look back at it, and the whole time I was there I was trying to fit in. I was trying to make people happy by working hard, never getting any recognition for my efforts. I know now that was totally wrong. I should have been playing for myself. I should have used that time for fun and growth, but I didn't.

This has continued throughout my musical life: all business. Play in this band with these guys. They're good. You'll get lots of gigs and make money.

Play with this guy, make him happy. Play with him and get in with his crowd of musicians. You'll get gigs, make money, and pay some bills.

This band needs a bass player. Leave your gig, go play with them. You'll be happy then. You'll make money.

This band needs a sub for a weekend. Learn their 50 tunes in three days. Impress them. Make money and get more calls because they like you so much that they'll tell their friends. "Darcy Patrick subbed for us. He was great. Hire him." That was my life for the past 30 years easy and it has to stop.

So now here I am sitting with this bass in my hand. I have no clue what to do with it!! I have no idea where to start and what to play. I have trained myself to just work on stuff and play for everyone else my whole musical life, just like I have been living for everyone else my entire life. And that was it! The trigger with music was the same trigger in the rest of my life. It was no secret, but I suddenly saw it, sitting with my bass on my lap and the music stand in front of me with books piled on it.

Being so depressed taught me what a dead end street it is to live for everyone else. Now I'm learning that the one thing I thought set me free was actually part of what was destroying me.

I had learned how to change my way of thinking and how to stop myself from spiralling, but how was I going to fix *this*? Where do I start? All I could do was sit and stare at the music stand with all those books on it. Books I bought so I could make other people happy by learning what was in them, so I could impress them with my talent. Not my talent to play music, but my talent to make people happy. To make them like me. So I grabbed all those books and put them away.

I began just like I did with my thought records: I started to practise, practise, practise. I picked up my Beatles fake book and started to work on chord melodies for *While My Guitar Gently Weeps* and *Here, There, and Everywhere*. I took my time and enjoyed doing it, planning each note and each harmony I played. I took the proper time to get it the way I like it to sound and then memorized those passages. I played them the way I wanted them to sound, getting out my feelings and making these songs mine. I gave them the proper time to sound good. Just like, when I write my thought records, I give my feelings and thoughts the attention they need. Learning to love yourself and enjoy yourself is a long battle and the more I played the more I noticed that time just flew by. One hour, two hours, three hours went by like nothing and I actually enjoyed myself playing my bass. I came up with some very good-sounding versions of these Beatle songs.

One day my next-door neighbour was outside. I asked her if I could play these songs I have worked so hard on for her. She said she would love to hear them, so I got my bass and my amp from my office and she sat in her chair on her back porch. I looked over at her and I was overcome with emotion. My neighbour Josie has cancer and we love her so much. She is part of our family and I just wanted to play for her and make her happy. I started to play and I started to cry! Playing meant something to me! I couldn't believe it. I wasn't empty. I wasn't spiralling at all. Every note I played had meaning and I loved what I was doing so much I was crying. I finished the first song and played the next one and the tears were pouring down my face. I finished those two songs and I was overwhelmed at the emotion I created in myself by just playing these songs. I asked Josie what she thought and she said that it was beautiful!! That she loved my playing and would love for me to play for her again.

I left for work with a smile on my face.

That moment changed the way I feel about playing music. I was overwhelmed by the fact that I could feel, after everything I have been through, being afraid to show emotion and the hard time I had going to my safe place and just letting go. Now it just pours out of me and I just let go! I don't go crazy and I am not afraid of it at all. I can embrace it and enjoy it. If music makes me feel this way then I need to give it another chance. I need to keep practising and learning to love it again.

I brought my bass on vacation for the first time in 10 years and played it every day. I enjoyed my time with it and all that was left to do was play a gig with the band and see what would happen. How would I deal with the triggers when they came up?

Journal entry

The first gig I did, I got to a little shit-hole of a bar and I was so nervous and shaking I almost cried while setting up the lights and the PA system. It was terrifying that it had come to this, with 30 years of gigging under my belt, but I was a mess just setting up to play with some good friends who didn't know what I was going thru. But I took a deep breath and embraced the fact that I was feeling these emotions and just battled on. I set up all the stuff and my good friend, the guitar player in the band, looked at me and extended his hand. I shook his hand and he said he was so happy to see me again after three weeks off. That brought a smile to my face and all was good.

I tried to not drink any beer but people started to buy for the band so I had one and it loosened me up a little. We sat together and started to talk. It had been 3 weeks since I had seen my band-mates. I wish I had the nerve to talk to the guitar player about what is going on with me, but that is the last thing I could do. He is one of my closest friends. He and his wife and kids are like family to me and my wife and son. I am so scared to actually talk to him about my depression and all I'm going through. I don't want to seem weak.

We started playing and my mind was all over the place. People were watching me and smiling and enjoying the music. I was thinking to myself, why are these people even here? I looked over at my good friend and all I could think was, I want tell him. I want to stop playing, but at the same time I don't want to let anyone down by doing that. But I wish I could. What a horrible night. Everything that I have worked for for so long and everything that I believed in was just gone. A wash-out. A complete and utter wash out!

I played that gig and I acted and I played a flawless night. I made the changes. I talked with people between sets. A good friend came out and saved me. He helped pass the time with me and made the night more enjoyable. But what was I going to do at the next gig? I can't let these gigs kill me every time I play. I work so hard during the week and I have made so much progress and I am enjoying life. How do I stop this spiralling at gigs? What do I do?

Journal entry from a gig.

I played my song in the first set. The first set was fun and I only had a slight slide. Working hard to stay up and keep a good outlook! Using my tools and they're working. I am fighting hard and kicking at the darkness.

Second set: the grand façade burns true. The house is packed and I bring my game up a level. The acting is thru the roof! The party is wild, people dancing and singing along. I am playing my ass off and yet I'm on the outside looking in! Just a passenger at this gig.

Third set, and the beer is flying. People are sending beer and shots to the band. I drink it and the spiral starts. Music is such a joke at this point. Years of practice and school, and all it leads to is me beating the shit out of my bass and playing my ass off and no one caring. I am playing lines that are insane, crossing bar lines, taking chances and killing it. Every note placed perfectly, voice leading to every chord change. Thinking eight bars a head at times and laughing at just how good I am playing. No one even notices.

No one even knows I am there.

I am a bass player. So lame and sad, but I am up and having fun. There is a difference tonight. I see that I am actually over-achieving and killing this gig. I am not a waste of flesh and I am not triggering thinking no one appreciates me or that I'm useless. I am far from that. I am killing it. And no one cares or even hears me.

I need to start playing for myself again, playing music that I love and that is challenging and makes me feel good about myself. I love this band and I love my band-mates. They are my closest friends and I will still play in this band but I need to have an outlet, a guilty-pleasure band, where I play the way I feel I should.

Tonight was a fight from start to finish but nothing comes without a fight so I have to keep playing and kicking at the darkness and the gigs will get better and better as I get stronger and stronger. Just like always practice and more practice. My life is one long fight on stage and off. That's just the way it is for me, but as long as I keep getting better and keep fighting then it's okay, because I am human. If I can overcome depression by fighting everyday then learning to love music will be the same fight. I will win.

Journal entry from a gig

I am sitting in a small bar, waiting for the band I am playing bass for tonight to show up. I feel really good tonight. I like subbing like this. I am playing and saving a gig that the band would have lost If I didn't agree to play. I am playing with young musicians who are in college right now, going through the same program I was in when I was their age. It's so exciting...

A 42 year old guy playing in a band with guys in their 20's is pretty cool. These guys were customers in the store when they were just young and still buy their stuff from us now.

Back when I was 22 they were just learning how to play. It's kind of cool to actually be playing with these guys. What a good vibe and what a fun time! The drummer was very good. I don't say that often. He was blown away that he actually got to play with me! How cool was that.

He said he always heard I was the best bass player in this area and that he never thought he would be so lucky to do a gig with me! He said that it is true I am as good and better than people say. He asked a lot of questions about college when I was going there and I was happy to answer his questions. He asked me how long I have been playing for, how long I had been gigging for and I smiled and answered all his questions. I just sat and talked with him about music and the business part of it and it was very cool. What a good night!

I left the gig happy and up and in a very good mood. I wish every gig was like this.

I used to think all the time when I would spiral when I wanted to disappear how nice it would be to leave everything behind and move to the top of mountain and cast away all my belongings and become a monk and just live a solitary life. How peaceful this would be no worries and nothing stressing me out.

I left the band I had with my close friends. The stress from performing live was too much I stopped taking on sub gigs I told everyone that I have retired form music for a short time I needed a break I have been playing professionally for over 30 years now.

After I did this and I gave myself a few days to just relax and think about why I left music. I started to feel real good I started to feel like I was that monk in the mountains who cast everything he owned away to better himself. I felt free like I was born again now if I wanted to play it was going to be for me and me alone I made a list of pros and cons for stopping playing music. Here is my list.

Stopping Playing music

Pros

- No more bad days after gigs
- I feel good about playing my bass again
- No more sleepless nights leading up to a gig I wish I never took
- More time spent with Sherri and Dylan
- When I play now I play for myself only
- I have stopped trying to make other people happy
- No more learning 50 tunes in a week
- No more calls from people who I don't want to play with
- No more looking for approval from band mates and no more spiraling on stage
- No more looking to the crowd and wondering if there watching and waiting for me to mess up a song
- Weekends off in summer!!
- Staying sober and not spiraling

Con's

- I will miss the extra money.....

This list surprised me I was taking away so many triggers by just leaving music. Treating myself good and actually living my life for myself.

I talked a lot at therapy about my years playing music, I took more than a couple weeks off playing my bass it was 4 months off. Not even looking at one or even touching one. My therapist wanted me to give playing another try but to work my way into it slowly to make my own beginning. Mastora told me to sit with my bass in the same room with me, on my back porch or on my patio. I would just look at it and think of only good memories I had when I was playing it.

So I let my bass hang out with me just sit there, I would looked at it and I would think about some pretty fun gig's I had with it and how I made this bass my own over time. Here is what I wrote in my journal one day when I was just sitting looking at my bass.

Journal entry Black bass:

My Black bass was my Groovy Food bass (Groovy Food is I band I played in for 3 years).It's a reissue of a 1962 jazz bass, The paint never cured properly and there are large chips of paint missing from the body. The largest one being where the large Groovy Food Sticker was once placed on the bass and I removed the sticker and most of the paint exposing the open wood grain very beautiful in a way. I took the finish off the back of the neck by sanding it by hand taking great care and time to do the best job I could. I then did a hand rubbed oil finish on the open wood, coat after coat taking great care and sanding after each dried coat till it felt like silk.

This bass plays like it is part of me an extension of my body. Musicians search and search for these types of instruments and I made this bass myself with the work I did to it! I used to say that my Black Bass always did what I told it to do because it was part of me. I used this bass exclusively with Groovy Food for 3 years, hard playing and so many gig's I couldn't begin to count. My heart and soul is all over this bass, Beat up and battered after so many gig's. All the steel is rusted on the bridge locking all the adjusting screws in place from the sweat and the beer and the shots of boozy spilt all over it there is no shinny finish left just a flat black. But still this beat up bass continues to play nice and sound incredible.

The action is so low and sweet just placing a finger on a string will fret a note and the bass will sing. Only I know how to make this bass play. When other people try to play the bass it just frets out and buzzes. I remember playing many open Mic Jams, where people come and are welcome to play with the band and guys would get up and try to play my bass and I would think to myself there is no way my bass is going to do what they want it to and they would play and it would buzz and sound just horrible. I can only play this bass me and only me it is part of me.

I am going to play this bass again someday when I am ready. My Black bass is so beautiful and has so many memories attached to it good ones that I never saw before. Rebuilding and growing as a musician is going to be a special thing and a personal thing as I have learned over the past 1 year fighting depression. I think my Black Bass and myself have an attachment to each other and I feel maybe we will both take this new path together. I will learn to love what I do, make real nice music and grow a passion for It. I know it will take time but I have nothing but time on my hands and at the wonderful age of 43 I am learning to be myself and what a accomplishment it is turning out to be. I think the icing on the cake will be me becoming the musician I have always wanted to be. Myself and my Black Bass just might end up on stage again! Who knows.

This was my new start a type of exposure therapy. I thought I could do it on my own and after I played for Josie that day I knew I was able to but I just needed the right tools and Mastora came through again.

I sat with my bass and listened to records outside on my patio. Beatle records my favourite band, Revolver, Rubber soul, Help, to list a few. Myself and my Black Bass became good friends listening buddy's you might say the more I hung out with my bass the more good memories I found from playing music ones I had never seen before the Vail was being lifted and I was starting to feel good about music again.

One morning on I run I decided to finally just say good bye to all the bad things I had connected to music this is how I did it. This is a email I sent to my therapist after a run and after I worked through and healed my past musical life.

Mastora,

I have something I would like to share with you I hope you don't mind. This is what I wrote in my Journal this morning and what I did on my run to heal the way I feel about music.

On my run this morning I said good bye to all the things that bothered me about playing music. When I said good bye I said hello to something positive.

I went through everything I wasn't afraid of saying out loud what I really felt about people I tried to please. Things I tried to do for them, Things that stressed me out and I lost sleep over I said good bye to it all and I said hello to happy things that I didn't let myself have before things I felt were out or reach or I didn't deserve to have. I let in all the good that I never had before.

It felt fantastic and good to just say all these things out loud and it was even better that I countered with what I want to feel now. I realized that this isn't me saying good bye to music but me actually just growing as a musician. I will now start over, I will look at my bass in a new way, I will learn to look at music in a new way just like I have learned to live my life in a new way.

New tools new outlook and new views. This is not the end of my musical career but an exciting new direction a new start! If I have my bass sitting in a room with me then I will let it sit and I will think about the good times I have had with it. I will also start by just seeing the beauty in the bass itself. If one day I pick it up and play it then that will be just fine but I am willing to take the time to let it happen.

I am willing to go even further then I have so far in my almost 2 years of fighting depression and learn to be a musician, I deserve to be happy! I deserve to now enjoy my talent for myself. I have given away too many years to other people's happiness and now I am ready to do it for myself.

I am working on my playing now I play for 5 minutes at a time and if I have any bad thoughts I stop and walk away I am accomplishing a lot with self love and realizing that it is okay to enjoy myself when I play my bass. I am a long way from doing a gig or joining a band but I am learning to be the musician I always wanted to be and that is what matters. I can say I have passion for music for the first time ever and it is exciting!

Depression

Just before we left on this vacation, Robin Williams ended his life. I remember lying in bed and my wife asked me how I felt about this happening seeing as he suffered from depression. I told my wife I felt horrible for his family and for him because depression won. The next day I had a therapy session and my therapist asked me what I thought about it as well. She told me that as soon as she heard about it she thought about me and how when I started seeing her I was in such bad shape. She thought about how I told her I was acting all the time, never really feeling and never really being myself. We talked in depth about how it might have been for Robin Williams, the funny man. We talked about depression and how it can affect even the most famous and rich people and if not treated it will kill you. We talked about the stigma attached to it and how people are so afraid to talk about it.

This is a Journal entry did about depression

Journal entry:

Depression

Depression is the most powerful, most consuming illness on earth. It is that way because it has no boundaries. It's so dangerous, even fatal if not treated right. It never goes away, but waits just out of sight, in the shadows. When you think you have it beat, it will work itself back into your life.

Depression doesn't care how smart you are or how many degrees you have, how you dress, or what part of town you live in. It doesn't care about how much money you have. Or how famous you are. Depression is the vilest thing ever. When it gets you, you keep it a secret and that makes it stronger and bigger and smarter.

There is such a stigma attached to depression that people will act like everything is okay while they're acting there dying inside. Depression grows and grows. You feel like an outcast and like there really is nowhere to turn as depression just smiles and sucks your soul out of you. People who don't know about it talk about it and make it worse. Depression is always working hard to bring you down all the time. It never stops.

To overcome depression is a nonstop fight. The only way to beat it is to fight it all the time, every day, depression loves it when people stay at home. People also keep to themselves and stop talking to their friends. Depression loves that, too. Depression loves it when people start drinking and taking drugs. Depression kills people and when it does, other people say that the person was a coward or that they took the easy way out. Other people who suffer from depression know that and so feel that they can never talk about it, which makes their problem even worse.

People with depression don't kill themselves. Depression kills them. They reach a point where they are so deep and so low with it, there is nowhere to turn. They are afraid to fight and do not know how to fight, and giving in seems so much easier. I used try to run from it that never worked. I sat in my office and cried, even walked out of the store. I was going to walk till I died one day.

Depression has taken so many lives and so many suffer in silence and the stigma behind it is so great that it seems like it will always win. I have suffered for over 38 years. I stood at the edge myself and I turned. I ran away and I learned to fight. I have tools that depression can't match. I practice every day and I fight everyday and I will win over time because I get stronger every day.

This is a great month for me. I celebrate it by taking pride in the fact I stood and fought .But there are so many people who have not taken the steps I have taken. That's why I am writing this book: to help people like me! If you are one of them, please make the call for help! Depression is killing so many people mentally and physically. It needs to be stopped.

Use the tools:

- Write every day to prove to yourself that those negative thoughts are wrong.
- Forgive yourself, and everyone else.
- Love yourself. Prove it by treating yourself well.
- Live in the moment
- Make affirmations: Write them and say them:
- I succeed in life
- I am worth changing
- I deserve to be happy.
- I am not afraid to be happy
- I am not afraid to be myself.
- I am a strong and smart person.
- I will beat depression.

Don't be afraid to talk to someone. You're not alone, no matter how lonely and empty you feel when the world closes in and you have nowhere turn or run. Pick up a phone, like I did, and make a call. It is so easy and it will change your life and make you strong. You will learn to fight this illness, get the proper help you need and the tools to live a happy life.

Learning that you are worth changing is so very important we all have the right to be happy, each and every one of us. Time invested in your self is never wasted. You are the most important person in your life. We will all make mistakes and we all have to admit we are human. Then we all have to forgive and forget.

I will say it again: forgive yourself.

Most of all, don't carry guilt around with you. It will bring you down. Enjoy life. Take chances and smile and laugh at your attempts that fall short. Fight depression at every turn. Take its power away. Fight and battle. Write and write, talk and talk. Stop acting like nothing is wrong when something *is* wrong. You can even sing my song lyric if you like. It will inspire you like it does me , If I am having a bad day sometimes I will sing it all day to remind myself that I have to fight and fight to live a happy life and be myself. "Nothing worth having doesn't come without some kind of fight..... You gotta kick at the darkness till it bleeds day light".

Yoga and meditation

In the winter months it is impossible to run at all on most days. My therapist was concerned that without physical exercise I would slip back into bad thought patterns and bad habits. Winter in Canada can cause depression even in the strongest person. Not being outside feeling the sun on your skin, just being stuck inside feeling trapped can be a horrible thing and trigger a spiral.

She told me I should take up yoga for many reasons. Physically it was good exercise and mentally it was calming. I thought I would give it try so I started off slow with 2 poses and held them for 30 seconds at a time. I searched the internet and soon my poses grew along with my flexibility and strength.

Before I knew it I was up to holding my posses for 2 mins at a time I had worked up a 2 hour routine. The calming state of mind is incredible every morning I would do my routine just like everything else I was tough to do. Practice, practice, and more practice. When I am doing Yoga the world just melts away and I found that I would have a much better start to my day clearing my head concentrating only on the posses and nothing else. I got stronger and stronger in mind and body I found that I got a better core work out then I ever did from sit ups and weight training .The whole treating myself with love started feeling natural and much easier after doing Yoga.

Paying attention to every move I made and controlling my body just added to the self love I was working toward. It is like petting a dog and getting to know that dog and growing a friend ship between mind and body .You make a connection with mind and body which you never had before.

Once the weather broke I was able to do my Yoga and run which was even better. I was able to do Yoga in my back yard beside my pond I changed how long I held my poses for so I could get a 8km run in at the half way point in the routine come home and finish the 2nd half before walking Dylan to school and going to work. Here is a journal entry from my first time doing Yoga outside.

Journal entry

This morning I took a little time to myself. I did yoga on my patio at water level beside my pond. I listened to my surroundings, my pond's water fall, birds chirping as the sun rouse, I went through all my poses and held them all for 2mins it was a full 2 hour routine.

It felt so good to be outside doing Yoga, I had thought about it many times while down stairs in my basement office during the cold winter. Seeing the blue sky above me and the clouds floating by being surrounded by nature was just breathtaking.

It felt so good to take this time out for myself to treat myself to this wonderful experience it is so important to just do simple things like Yoga and feel the happiness which it brings. I am learning so much about life and how important happiness is to live a health life. There are no life threatening things happening to me, no matters in my life that have to be dealt with. I will live and enjoy life, be happy and learn everyday just what it means to be happy and learn there is nothing that needs to be done. My happiness is truly what matters. I look forward to the days that come. The many times I will sit and do my Yoga beside my pond this spring and summer.

- I succeed in life
- I am worth changing
- I deserve to be happy, I am not afraid to be happy
- I am not afraid to be myself
- I am a strong and smart man I will beat depression.

Now my day just doesn't feel right if I don't start it out with Yoga. Now that the weather is good I run as well. I am learning so much and growing as a person and finding happiness!

Meditation:

In therapy we started to work on many types of mediation to help me stay calm when a tough situation would arrive or when I just needed to relax. Since now I was able to go to my safe place without any problems. Mastora added a wonderfull meditation.

She told me to sit comfortably and just breathe deep and naturally, just take notice of how my body felt my arms and my legs just relax and empty my mind.

Now I was to picture what emotion I felt and make it into a large object any shape or thing I wished it to be. I pictured a large glowing ball just in front me it was big and hot! She now told me to take my hands and bring them up to the ball and place them on each side of the ball. Imagine that I can bring my hands together and shrink this ball into a small object that could fit into the palm of my hand. I turned this large ball into a tinny cloud which just sat in the middle of the palm of my left hand. Now she said make that object disappear in any way you would like, maybe just close your hand and squeeze it until there is nothing left. I chose to shine sun light on this cloud and just make it slowly disappear into nothing. This meditation was fantastic and just proved to me any emotions in life that are playing on my mind can just be shrunk down to nothing and I can make them disappear and calm my mood. Like I said before nothing in my life is life threatening or needs to be dealt with any state of urgency. I alone control my moods and emotions and this was just another tool for me to use. This is a journal entry I made on a run so I would have lots of different things to turn the negative emotions into when I did this Meditation.

Journal entry

This morning on my run I thought about soft harmless things for my new meditation I was taught to use at my last session.

A tiny feather that sits in the palm of my hand and is lighter than air. With a tiny breath it can float out of my hand and get taken away by a gentle breeze.

Dry sand running threw my fingers and just disappearing into nothing.

Holding a dead dandy lion and blowing it with my breath and sending the seeds flying away in a warm summer breeze.

A nice soft leaf from a lavender plant holding it between my thumb and finger, slowly rubbing it and releasing its wonderful scent into the air and just dropping it after I am done.

After my run I was relaxed and slowly walked home and was at peace, smiling and feeling proud of myself for what I had accomplished on this run I now had I lot of images to use in my meditation. The fact that my run itself was like a meditation of its own was even better.

I started to create my own meditations as well as time went by. I am able to bring back wonderful images from runs , plus beautiful things I have seen or done. I just sit on my Yoga mat and I breathe deep and I think of something that was just beautiful in my mind and I go there. Here is a journal entry where I did just that.

Journal entry

As I sit on my yoga mat and breathe deep on this cold March day with a freezing rain warning in effect. I bring myself back to the end of a run I had on vacation at Sauble Beach one summer.

At the end of the run I sat on the beach and crossed my legs, I looked out at the beautiful blue sky and the clouds slowly moving, crystal clear water , golden sand and I listened to the calm water wash up on the shore. I let the world fade away and the morning sun warm my face and body as I closed my eyes. I just took deep breathes and lived in the moment. I let the sound of the water wash me away and think of nothing but my deep breathing and getting lost in this wonder place.

How lucky I was to have such a wonderful thing to remember, to write about it and use it as a place to go to in a meditation is fantastic. To use it on such a dark and grey day in March is even better a perfect way to start my day happy and relaxed!

Yoga and Meditation are playing a huge role in my fight against depression just starting a day out right happy and relaxed is such a big thing. I think of it as eating a good breakfast first thing in the morning people say it is the most important meal of the day. I say being happy and relaxed is a good start along with a good breakfast.

I will end a run with a 5min long meditation. During yoga I will think of a beautiful place and take myself there. At the end of hard day I will sit at my pond and let myself drift away till everything is out of my mind. Meditation is a wonderful tool ,paired with yoga and my runs I am at peace mind and body.

1 year celebration

I am leaving on vacation Saturday morning. It has been 1 full year since I made the call and took the first step towards changing my life and getting better and living my dream of being myself.

Last year at this time I was a complete mess. I would spiral every day and want to disappear. When I look back at those days, they seem so far away from me as I sit here and write this book.

Today is a celebration and I am beaming with pride at who I have become! I am strong and I am a hard worker who never stops trying to be the best I can be. I know I will have bad days and I know I'll have problems and I know I will spiral. But I also know I have the tools to stop and to overcome.

I write every day. I acknowledge the feelings I have and I let them in and I feel them!

- It is okay to feel good or bad.
- It is okay to be happy.
- It is okay to forgive.
- It is okay to live in the moment.
- It is okay to let people and things go.
- It is okay to leave work at work.
- It is okay to believe in yourself.

- It is okay to love who you are.
- It is okay to be myself.

Journal entry

Anniversary

Today I am overcome with emotion. Happiness is filling me up and I am brought to tears in my office. Tears of joy, tears of happiness! What a change I am feeling in my life to feel emotion in a good way and be brought to tears over it!

I am accepting the happy feelings and it is breathtaking, to say the least. I am filled with joy over the anniversary of meeting my son. I am also proud of myself for making the call and getting help working so hard and learning so much and fighting to beat depression. "I am a strong and smart man " I believe it in my heart to day!!

I am also proud of myself for not jumping that day and I have forgiven myself for what I was going to do. I am overjoyed today! The first two weeks of August are such a special time.

Journal entry

My run while I was on vacation:

Today, while I ran, the water wasn't even moving. As I ran I could see the beautiful blues and greens of the water and the golden sand which appears so bright through the water. As I ran, I thought about nothing and just marveled at this beautiful sight I was so lucky to see on this morning.

I saw a sand bank right at the shore, which I normally would not see because of the waves crashing on the shore. But today I saw it and I jumped over the water and landed on the sand bank and ran on it. It felt so good having the water go between my toes. It was cold and about two inches deep. I ran along this sand bar for 200 meters. I could feel the water and the sand perfectly moving between my toes the feeling was incredible. I looked over and realized that I was 20 feet out into the lake, still running on this sand bank gutting out deeper and deeper but I was running in just 2 inches of water still. When I jumped off the sand bank I was in knee high water. It was fantastic. I ran through the water, never breaking my stride, and got back to the land. As I ran I thought to myself, I may be broke and I may have used up my line of credit but that was one of the richest experiences I have ever had. I am a rich man. I have a beautiful son and beautiful wife and I get to run along this fantastic beach twelve times a year for the last eight years. No one can take that away from me ever, no matter how much debt I have. I am on holiday's being paid by Long and McQuade for the hard work I do. Life sounds pretty good to me right now. I finished my run and walked back to the cottage nice and slow, relaxed and happy.

Even during this time of celebration, and while feeling so proud of my progress, I am learning that there is no break from depression. Even on vacation with my family, depression doesn't take time off. As hard as I tried for three days, I ended up having to write thought records. There is no shame in that. I talked with Mastora about it and she was impressed that I lasted those three days and that I didn't write sooner. She told me that these tools need to be used all the time and that people actually keep diaries from the time they are just little children. These tools are lifelong tools. I was kind of taken aback a little because I had thought that at some time in my life I would be able to stop writing these records. But it is okay. If I need to keeping using these tools forever and ever that is okay, because you see it is much better to write down my thoughts than it is to spiral down and let depression back into my life.

When I run now

When I run now, it is a special time for me. Gone are the runs of hate and the runs of worry and self loathing. These runs have been replaced by runs of hope, during which I think about good things. Good things I have done and good things that will come from all my hard work.

When I run, I look around at all the beauty that I never saw before. I see trees, flowers, birds, and clouds. I marvel at the sunrise and the colours that are created in the morning sky. I get lost in the moment and let time pass. This is my time, my run, and my way of enjoying myself!

I don't run myself into the ground anymore. When I feel good I am in no hurry. I slow down and take it easy. I want this 5km or 10 or 12 km run to last. I want to enjoy each step. I want to feel the sidewalk under my feet and to smell the morning air. I want to run my hand over the fresh growth of a bush as I run past. I love to pull a leaf off a tree and feel it between my fingers. The 21 km runs are gone. No more long beat-myself-up runs. I try to run every day. I want to run into my 60's and 70's. I want live and love life as long as I can, and if that means fighting every day then I am ready for that fight.

I want to think about nice things and let those thoughts fill me with emotion. I want to smile and I even want cry! I want to feel life, the good and the bad. I want to imagine things and get lost in those images. I want to run and think about nothing and if I want to I will go to my safe place and walk inside a tree and just stay there for a while. I'll do it. I do it all the time.

Nothing touches me when I run now, unless I wish it to. I alone control my emotions and how I feel. I worry about nothing and I never think of the past in a bad way. I remember good things now. My life has good memories as well, not just bad.

If some asks me now "Why do you run?", "What are you running from?" I have new answers for them, new and exciting answers!

"Why do you run?"

I run for the enjoyment of life. Some people paint, some people garden, some people meditate or go for walks, read books, even play music. I run because I love to do so, and I enjoy doing what I love. Do you do anything you truly love in life? What is it? Tell me all about it. If you don't have something, I'll teach you how to run if you like.

"What are you running from?"

I am running from nothing. I stopped running from things last year. I turned and ran towards the problem. I learned to fight it and win my life back. I used to run from depression. I don't run from it anymore. I fight it.

I run now because I love to. Some day, when my body is not capable of running anymore, I will have so many good memories of when I was able to run that I will just sit and smile and remember all the beautiful things I saw on my runs when I was a young man.

In the end

As I finish writing this book I am overcome with emotion, which is an incredible feeling! I am finished acting like I am happy I am learning to be happy and be myself a lifelong goal. I am using my tools everyday to fight and to beat depression "Kicking at the darkness till it bleeds daylight". I feel so proud and happy that I can share my story about how I have learnt to fight this horrible illness. I say fight because it is a lifelong fight, against an illness that is never cured. I hope that what I have written helps people like me. I hope that it also opens a few eyes about depression and helps kill the stigma attached to it.

Depression is real and it kills. When you feel you have nowhere to turn and the blinders go on and you spiral down to the bottom like I used to, and you just want to disappear, pick up the phone and call for help. Doing that will take all the courage you have, but it is worth it. You are worth changing and you can change. If I can, so can you.

Please remember the tools I talked about. I can't repeat them enough.

Make the call for help! Talk to someone! My therapist saved my life. There are even distress lines you can call when you are in a bad place and you have no one to reach out to. Call a friend – they love you and they will help you just by talking to you.

Write things down. Journal every day, and read what you write and try to see what triggered you. Do thought records and prove your negative thoughts wrong whenever you can. Be honest and stop acting and be yourself.

Treat yourself well. Take time just for yourself. Go for a walk or a run. Learn to love yourself and give yourself time away from the world, where you can just think about nothing. Get lost in the moment. Take joy doing simple things: colour, play with toys, buy some Lego and play with it!!

Make affirmations for yourself and say them every day. Write them in your journal like I do. Believe them and love them and be proud of who you are.

Don't live in the past. Forgive and forget. And the most important thing you can do is forgive yourself and live life and be happy. To forgive is divine.

Practice, practice, practice. What seems like hard work now will become second nature as time passes and you get stronger.

Live life and love life and be strong and fight every day. I do. I will never stop fighting. I love who I am and I will never stop working on my lifelong dream to one day be myself!!!

I have saved a few Thought records and journal entries for the end of the book. These are my favorite ones. They are very inspiring. Enjoy them and enjoy life, because that's what life is for!

Thought record:

On my run this morning.

I am so proud of myself today and I am not afraid to show it. I am happy and proud. This morning on my run I spent my time in my safe place.

Moods:

Relaxed 100%, happy 100%

Sit:

I went to my safe place. My safe place is a tree. I imagined that I was a tall tree planted in my parents' back yard. My father's Ginkgo tree he planted when I was just six years old. I breathed deeply, inhaling through my leaves and exhaling through my roots. I just relaxed and did this for quite a while. Just thinking about what it must be like to be a tree. Not to have any expectations or worries, to have nothing to do but grow and grow, because I am a tree and that's what trees do.

I picture my father as a strong, young man planting me with his strong and caring, gentle hands. They are the same strong hands that held me as a baby and rocked me to sleep. They rocked my six older brothers as well. I think about how my father would water me after work and just stand there watching everyday as I grew.

As this tree I also watch a family grow around me never wanting to interfere or pass judgment or criticize, wanting only to breathe deeply and grow nice and slow, and watch this family grow as well. I watch soccer games. I watch this strong man build tree houses for his sons. I watch him play baseball with them and even build a pool and ice rinks for hockey games.

All along, my branches just grew and grew. I got taller and taller, children turned to teens and teens turned to men. The man who was once so strong also got older and older, and became a grandfather.

As a tree time, must be a very peaceful thing. As a tree, I just watch life flow by, with no obligations and no commitments. I just grow and learn just like I am doing in real life, growing and learning how to be myself. I love my safe place and I love who I am.

This was a goal I had made ever since I started therapy and found my safe place, which was not an easy task at the time. Now I am proud of myself, which is something I really haven't been able to say ever. I am proud because I did this. I reached a meditative state went to my safe place ran 8km in my safe place my tree. I am proud of myself because I have this safe place I can go to. I am worth changing and I am not afraid to be myself.

I feel good about myself!

Thought record:

My run

This morning on my run, I took the time to lose myself and look at the beauty all around.

Moods:

Happy 100% Relaxed 90%

I looked at all the beautiful trees and their wonderful shapes and vibrant colours. The light greens, the dark greens, the reds, the browns and how alive they were. How different and unique each tree is: the shapes of their trunks and the flowers on the flowering trees. The bright pink and red colours of a cherry tree in the spring. The beautiful white snowball bushes as well. The wonderful smell of blooming lilacs and lavender.

I got a little selfish and pictured myself in one of these vibrant trees and how it must feel to be inside one bursting with life after a long winter and the exhilaration of flowering. It was fantastic. I also pulled a leaf off a tree and ran it between my fingers feeling its veins and its unique texture

I also ran past bushes and ran my hand over top of the new growth and felt the energy each bush had.

I looked up at the clouds and saw the beauty in the sunrise and marveled at the colours that the sun and clouds were making together: the reds, the pinks, and the blue sky framing it all. It was just breathtaking.

I had a great 12 km run, and when I finished, I walked for 1 km and just breathed deeply and relaxed. I was amazed at how good I felt. 12km and it felt like I had not even run at all.

This is a good thought record who says they all have to be bad!!

On the beach, 2014

On the beach holding my wife's hand watching my son play in the sand and waves. I am filled with joy. I feel it in my heart. Last year I was sitting in the same place and I was crying and spiraling every day. I had nowhere to turn and no way of helping myself. I broke down in front of my wife for the first time, crying and shaking and wanting to disappear. Today I am strong and I have the tools to fight every day and win. I am so proud of myself today, holding my wife's hand and loving life.

What a difference from last year. I live in the moment. I take joy in small things. I love life and I do not want disappear at all. I have fought and fought and I deserve to me happy. I am worth changing and I love this life I have. Even with the work I have to do every day, and even with these thought records I do, I wouldn't have it any other way. Living and loving, forgiving and fighting, and holding my wife's hand on this beautiful beach, together as a family.

I am going to grow old with my wife and watch my son grow into a man and someday I'll hold a grandchild of my own. I am up for the fight. I hope depression is because I will beat it every day if I have to!

Mind

my story
is not yet
told.

Body

soul

Dave Petrits

CPSIA information can be obtained
at www.ICGtesting.com
Printed in the USA
LVHW010638060919
630126LV00005B/49